Mastering Correction of Accounting Errors

by

Sharon H. Fettus, Ph.D., CPA
Assistant Professor
Department of Economics and Business
The Catholic University of America
Washington, D.C.

Mary D. Myers, MBA, Ph.D., CPA
Professor of Accounting
College of Business
Shippensburg University
Shippensburg, Pennsylvania

Sharon H. Fettus, Ph.D., CPA, is an Assistant
Professor in the Department of Economics and
Business at The Catholic University of America,
Washington, D.C. She has published in both
academic and practice-oriented journals.

Mary D. Myers, MBA, Ph.D., CPA, is Professor of
Accounting in the College of Business at Shippensburg
University, Shippensburg, Pennsylvania. She has
published in both academic and professional journals.

©AIPB, 2007
ISBN 1-884826-26-1

This publication is designed to provide accurate and authoritative information in regard to the subject matter
covered. It is sold with the understanding that the publisher and author are not engaged in rendering legal,
accounting or other professional services. If legal advice or other expert assistance is required, the services of
a competent professional person should be sought.—From a Declaration of Principles jointly adopted by a
Committee of the American Bar Association and a Committee of Publishers and Associations.

INTRODUCTION

Mastering Correction of Accounting Errors covers everything you need to know for the error correction and bank reconciliation portion of the *Certified Bookkeeper* examination. If you take the optional open-book Final Examination at the end of this workbook, return the answer sheet to AIPB and achieve a grade of at least 70, then become a *Certified Bookkeeper* within three years, you will receive retroactively seven (7) Continuing Professional Education Credits (CPECs) toward the *Certified Bookkeeper* continuing education requirements. You will also receive promptly an AIPB *Certificate of Completion.*

If you are not an applicant for the *Certified Bookkeeper* designation and take the optional open-book Final Examination at the end of this workbook, return the answer sheet to AIPB and achieve a grade of at least 70, you will receive an AIPB *Certificate of Completion.*

Upon completing this course, you should be able to:

1. perform the monthly bank reconciliation and find and correct errors revealed by it;

2. find and correct errors in the trial balance;

3. find and correct accrual errors discovered before the books are closed; and

4. find and correct deferral errors discovered before the books are closed.

The course does not deal with errors caused by fraud or gross negligence.

Important: Throughout the course, tax effects are ignored.

To get the most out of the course, we suggest the following:

1. Read the concise narrative that begins each section.

2. Read the section narrative again. This time, cover the solution to each problem and try to figure it out. *Actually write it out.* By simply *trying* to solve the problem and checking your answer against the correct solution, you will learn a great deal.

3. Take Quiz #1 at the end of each section to see what you learned or need to review.

4. Take Quiz #2 at the end of each section to master any points previously missed.

Lastly, please take a moment to fill out and send in the *Course Evaluation* at the back (whether or not you take the final exam). It will help us to improve this and other courses.

We want to thank the people whose hard work contributed to this workbook, including Supervisory Editor L.G. Schloss, Department of Accounting and Law (retired), Iona College, New Rochelle, New York; Joanne Brodsky for proofreading; and typesetter Mary Beth Mason, WordMason, Inc., Silver Spring, Maryland.

Thank you, enjoy the course—and congratulations on taking a major step toward advancing your professional knowledge and career.

CONTENTS

Certified Bookkeeper Applicants

The best way to study for the certification exam is to take each section's quizzes over and over until you can answer questions quickly and comfortably—*and* know why the answer is correct. If you have trouble with a question, or know the answer, but not why it is correct, review the related material. Write answers on a separate sheet, wherever possible, to avoid seeing them each time you take the quiz.

WHERE ERRORS OCCUR
AND HOW THEY ARE FOUND

Introduction

What is an accounting error? An *accounting error* is defined as the "incorrect recording and reporting of facts about the business that existed at the time an event or transaction was recorded."[1]

Many accounting errors are prevented by basic double-entry bookkeeping, which keeps the books in "balance" by requiring that debits equal credits in each entry. Other errors are prevented—or discovered—by internal controls. Internal controls assure the reliability of accounting information through procedures such as bank reconciliations and preparation of trial balances. But even with the best controls, the books may contain errors. When an error occurs, accounting personnel responsible for correcting the error must find it, identify the amount of the error, the accounts it affects, and in what period the error was made: the current period, the year before or several years before.

Types of Errors

Accounting errors are often caused by simple accounting mistakes or employee oversight, such as forgetting to record an event. These errors are easier to find when you know what to look for. Various types of accounting errors include:

- *Omission (failing to record an event),* such as not recording a return of merchandise.

- *Accrual or deferral error,* such as accruing or deferring the wrong amount or failing to make the accrual or deferral.

- *Classification error,* such as debiting a rent payment to Insurance Expense instead of to Rent Expense.

---

1. Welsh, Newman and Zlatkovich, *Intermediate Accounting*, 8th Ed. (Homewood, Ill.: Irwin, 1989): p. 1267.

- **Arithmetic mistake,** such as an incorrect total on an inventory tally sheet.

- **Use of an incorrect accounting principle,** such as expensing an equipment purchase instead of capitalizing it.

- **Use of an improper estimate,** such as using an allowance for doubtful accounts estimate of 2% of sales when it should be 4% of sales.

- **Transposition (reversal of two digits in a number),** such as recording $83 as $38.

- **Slide (the decimal point has been put in the wrong place),** such as recording $250 as $25 or as $2,500.

- **Posting error,** such as crediting Cash[2] for a sale instead of debiting it.

Finding Accounting Errors

Most accounting errors are found during routine activities.

- **Monthly bank reconciliation.** Each month, the Cash account is reconciled with the monthly bank statement. Most discrepancies between the end-of-month bank balance and Cash account balance are caused by differences in timing. Items recorded in Cash may not be on the bank statement. Such items include *deposits in transit—* (deposits sent in at the end of the month after the bank has prepared the monthly statement) and *checks outstanding* (payments made by the company that have not cleared the bank).

Similarly, items on the bank statement may not yet be recorded in Cash, such as *interest earned on the checking account balance*, *bank fees* and *NSF* (not sufficient funds) *checks.*

- **Preparation of the trial balance.** Most businesses periodically prepare a trial balance. It verifies that all ledger accounts for the period are in balance—that is, that total ledger account debits equal total ledger account credits.

---

2. In this section, the term "Cash," "Cash account" or "books" stands for the ledger Cash account.

- *Review of periodic adjustments to the accounts.* For example, when reviewing the adjusting entries, you might discover that depreciation expense was omitted for the company computer, machine, auto, or other asset, or that an incorrect amount was recorded.

- *Routine internal audits.* The accounting department makes periodic reviews to assure the reliability of accounting procedures, data and information.

- *Year-end financial audit.* This is performed by external auditors (auditors chosen "at arm's length") who examine the data reported on the financial statements and require corrections of any accounting errors to assure that the financial statements are fairly presented.

In addition, errors are sometimes discovered simply by chance.

Deciding How to Correct an Error

The correction of an error is determined by which accounts are affected and when the error was found (in the year the error was made, in the following year, or two or three years later).

For example, you discover at year end 20X1 that depreciation was understated by $3,000.

If the error was made *and* discovered in 20X1, it can be corrected merely by increasing both depreciation expense and accumulated depreciation by $3,000. This section explains how to make these corrections.

If, however, the 20X1 error is not discovered until 20X2, after the 20X1 books are closed, you cannot increase 20X1 depreciation expense because the 20X1 Depreciation Expense account has been closed out along with the other revenue and expense accounts. Instead, the solution will be a prior period adjustment to the opening balance of 20X2 Retained Earnings. Prior period adjustments are beyond the scope of this course.

Summary

Despite the safeguards provided by double-entry accounting and internal controls, errors occur. Errors may be uncovered during routine accounting procedures such as the periodic bank reconciliation, end-of-period account adjustments and internal and external audits. The key to finding errors is knowing their possible causes.

QUIZ 1   WHERE ERRORS OCCUR AND HOW THEY ARE FOUND

Problem I.

Multiple choice. Circle the correct answer.

1. Internal accounting controls . . .

   a. are part of every company's accounting system
   b. prevent accounting errors
   c. guarantee reliable accounting information
   d. help to ensure the reliability of accounting information

2. Which of the following is *not* used to detect accounting errors?

   a. monthly bank reconciliations
   b. prior period adjustments
   c. monthly trial balances
   d. internal audits

3. If depreciation expense of $1,000 is posted as $100, this is . . .

   a. a transposition error
   b. a classification error
   c. a slide error
   d. use of an incorrect accounting principle

4. If a company calculates bad debt expense at 1% of sales but the percentage used was 5% of sales, this is . . .

   a. a transposition error
   b. use of an improper estimate
   c. a slide error
   d. use of an incorrect accounting principle

5. SiliCo painted its building at a cost of $10,000 and decided to capitalize it (debit Buildings), instead of expensing it (debit Repairs and Maintenance Expense). This is . . .

    a. a transposition error
    b. a classification error
    c. an improper estimate
    d. use of an incorrect accounting principle

Problem II.

Fill in the blanks.

1. A $300 payment of an electric bill debited to Cash is a(n) _____ error.

2. The correction of an error is determined by which _____ are affected and _____ the error was found.

3. The _____ _____ helps to reveal errors by verifying that total _____ _____ debits and credits are in balance.

4. Errors may be uncovered in the year-end financial audit by the _____ _____.

Problem III.

List three routine accounting procedures during which accounting errors may be discovered.

1. _____

2. _____

3. _____

Problem IV.

Name seven common types of accounting errors.

1. _____

2. _____

3. _____

4. _____

5. _____

6. _____

7. _____

QUIZ 1   Solutions and Explanations

Problem I.

1. d

2. b

3. c
   This is a slide error because the decimal point has been moved one digit to the left.

4. b

5. d

Problem II.

1. posting

2. accounts; when

3. trial balance; ledger accounts

4. external auditor

Problem III.

Any three of the following five are correct:

1. monthly bank reconciliation

2. preparation of the trial balance

3. review of periodic adjustments to the accounts

4. routine internal audits

5. year-end financial audit

Problem IV.

Any seven of the following nine are correct:

1. omission (failing to record an event)

2. accrual or deferral error

3. classification error

4. arithmetic mistake

5. use of an incorrect accounting principle

6. use of an improper estimate

7. transposition

8. slide

9. posting error

QUIZ 2   WHERE ERRORS OCCUR AND HOW THEY ARE FOUND

Problem I.

Multiple choice. Circle the correct answer.

1. Which of the following is *not* an accounting error?

    a. failure to post an entry to the proper account
    b. failure to post the proper amount to an account
    c. failure to record a customer's payment
    d. failure to record that a bill has been contested by a customer

2. Your company's payment of $500 was debited to Cash. This is . . .

    a. a posting error
    b. a classification error
    c. an arithmetic mistake
    d. a slide

3. A rent payment check issued for $450 was recorded as a credit to Cash for $540. This is . . .

    a. a slide
    b. an incorrect account classification
    c. an arithmetic mistake
    d. a transposition error

4. CabotCo's accountant forgot to record annual interest expense. This is . . .

    a. a transposition error
    b. an arithmetic mistake
    c. use of an incorrect accounting principle
    d. an accrual error

Problem II.

Fill in the blanks.

1. An accounting error is defined as the incorrect _____ and _____ of facts about the business that existed at the time a(n) _____ or _____ was recorded.

2. Most differences between the end-of-month bank balance and cash account balance are caused by differences in _____.

3. An error in depreciation expense is likeliest to be discovered when _____ are made to the accounts.

Problem III.

Name three specific accounting activities that may uncover errors.

1. _____

2. _____

3. _____

QUIZ 2   Solutions and Explanations

Problem I.

    1. d

    2. a

    3. d

    4. d

Problem II.

    1. recording; reporting; event; transaction

    2. timing

    3. adjustments

Problem III.

    Any three of the following six is correct:

    1. Monthly bank reconciliation

    2. Preparation of the trial balance

    3. Review of periodic adjustments to the accounts

    4. Routine internal audits

    5. Year-end financial audit

    6. By chance

THE BANK RECONCILIATION

Introduction

Most companies verify at least monthly that the balances in their Cash[1] and bank accounts are correct by comparing them. The end-of-month balances in the bank and Cash account are rarely equal because of timing differences. For example, checks written recently will not have been paid by the bank and will not appear on the current bank statement. Similarly, bank fees for the month that appear on the bank statement will not yet be recorded in the Cash account. The process of bringing the bank and Cash accounts into balance is called the *bank reconciliation*.

If there is a separate Cash account for each bank account (and there should be), a reconciliation is done for each bank and corresponding Cash account. The bank reconciliation serves three major purposes:

> 1. to review information needed to bring company accounting records up to date at the end of the month or other period;

> 2. to verify that the ledger Cash account balance at the end of the month or other period is accurate and to correct any errors; and

> 3. to verify that the checking account balance at the end of the month or other period is accurate and to alert the bank of any errors.

It should be noted that this section does not deal with reconciling the company checkbook; it deals with reconciling the Cash account. Therefore, only the bank statement and the ledger Cash account are discussed, not the company checkbook.

Debits and Credits: Bank v. Company

Cash deposits in the company checking account are an asset for the company, but a liability for the bank. When the company increases Cash with a debit,

---

1. In this section, the term "Cash," "Cash account" or "books" refers to the ledger Cash account.

the bank increases its liabilities with a credit. For this reason, when the bank pays interest on the company's checking account balance or corrects an error in the company's favor, it issues a *credit memo* (and *credits* the company's bank account) and the company *debits* Cash.

Similarly, when the bank deducts a fee from the company checking account, it issues a *debit memo* (and *debits* the account) and the company *credits* Cash.

Why Company Bank and Cash Accounts Differ

The following discrepancies between bank and book accounts are the result of disbursements or receipts recorded on different dates by the company and bank.

Receipts and disbursements *recorded on the company books* but not recorded on the most recent bank statement. These include:

- *Deposits in transit.* These are deposits made by mail or in a night deposit lock box not yet recorded on the bank statement used in the reconciliation.

- *Undeposited cash.* Many businesses record receipts daily but make deposits at the bank only once or twice a week.

- *Outstanding checks.* The company paid bills, credited them to Cash and recorded the amount in the company checkbook, but the checks have not been paid by the bank, so they are not deducted on the current bank statement.

Receipts and disbursements *recorded by the bank* but not yet recorded on the company books. These include:

- *Credit memoranda.* These are additions to the company bank balance such as funds wired directly into the company account, notes collected by the bank on the company's behalf, interest earned on the checking account average balance, and cash transferred into the company account when a credit line is activated.

- *Debit memoranda.* These deductions from the company bank account include bank service charges, NSF (not sufficient funds) checks, and fees for items such as certified checks and safe-deposit boxes.

- *Authorized payments by the bank to a third party.* An example of this payment is the automatic lease payments that the bank deducts from the company account.

Errors in bank or company records. For example, the company or bank recorded payments or deposits for an incorrect amount in the wrong account.

The Step-by-Step Bank Reconciliation

The bank reconciliation is a two-part process. The bank balance and ledger Cash account are adjusted and reconciled to each other.

Part I: Reconciling the End-of-Month Bank Balance

1. *If cancelled checks are returned by the bank, put them in numerical order.*

2. *Examine each canceled check.* See that it is your company's, that it is drawn on the proper bank account, that it is properly signed, and that it is for the amount shown on the bank statement and in the Cash account. Make a list of outstanding checks by number and amount.

3. *Verify that deposit amounts listed on the bank statement conform to the deposit amounts on the company deposit slips and in the company Cash account.* Verify that deposits in transit that were missing from the previous month's bank statement are recorded on the current one. If they are not, track them down.

4. *Begin with the end-of-month bank balance.*

5. <u>Add</u>:

+ cash on hand (cash awaiting deposit,);

+ deposits in transit for the month covered by the bank statement.

6. <u>Deduct</u>:

– checks outstanding; investigate checks outstanding for more than a month or two.

7. *Add to or deduct from the bank statement balance the amount of any bank errors.* These may include a check from another company deducted from your bank statement, a numerical error, or the wrong amount listed for a deposit or check.

When you have completed this computation, reconcile the ledger Cash account.

Part II: Reconciling the Cash Account

8. *Begin with the end-of-month ledger Cash account balance.*

9. *Add credit memoranda*, such as:

+ amounts from funds wired directly into the company account;

+ received from the bank and not recorded by the company in the Cash account.

+ notes collected by the bank on the company's behalf;

+ interest earned on the average checking account balance;

+ cash transferred into the company account if a credit line was activated.

10. *Deduct debit memoranda for amounts not recorded by the company,* such as:

– bank service charges;

– NSF (nonsufficient funds or "bounced") checks;

– certified checks;

– safe-deposit box fees;

– other bank fees.

11. *Add to or deduct from the Cash account balance the amount of any errors made by the company*. These may be a numerical error or a check or deposit that was not recorded or was recorded for the wrong amount. You now have the adjusted Cash account balance.

The adjusted ledger Cash account balance should equal the adjusted bank balance. When they are equal, we say they are "reconciled" with each other.

12. *Record the journal entries for each adjustment to Cash and for any book errors*.

13. *Notify the bank of any bank errors*.

The bank reconciliation is now complete. The following examples illustrate how a bank reconciliation is performed.

Bank Reconciliation Example 1:
Reconciling the ledger Cash account
and the bank statement when there
are no errors

Figure 2-1 (page 18) may be copied for convenience. It gives the data you need to reconcile Tower Company's bank statement and Cash account as of May 31. It includes Tower's April bank reconciliation.

Part I: Adjusting Tower's Bank Balance

1. *If cancelled checks have been returned by the bank, put them in numerical order*. Assume this has been done. You note that check #715 is outstanding.

2. *Examine each canceled check*. Assume that each check has been verified as Tower's and as having been drawn on the proper bank account and is properly signed. Make sure that the amount of each check on the bank statement matches the amount in Tower's Cash account.

3. *Verify that the deposit amounts listed on the bank statement conform to deposit amounts on Tower's deposit slips (not shown) and on the deposits listed in Tower's Cash account*. You note that the bank has not recorded the May 31 deposit of $800.

Figure 2-1
Tower Company Bank Reconciliation as of April 30

Balance per bank statement, April 30	$1,050
Add: April 30 deposit in transit	350
	1,400
Deduct: Outstanding check #706	400
Corrected cash balance	$1,000
Balance per books, April 30	$1,005
Add: Interest	7
	1,012
Deduct: Service charges	12
Corrected cash balance, April 30	$1,000

Tower Company Cash Account for the Month Ended May 31

	Cash Receipts		Cash Disbursements	
			Check No.	
May 1 Balance		$1,000	707	$ 150
			708	700
6	2,300		709	120
10	50		710	340
14	650		711	980
20	1,500		712	70
31	800		713	630
Total receipts		5,300	714	170
		6,300	715	510
			716	260
May 31 Balance		$2,370	Total Disbursements	$3,930

Cash on hand (undeposited), $50

Bank Statement for Tower Company

Date	Check #	Debits	Credits	Balance
May 1				$1,050
2	706	$400	$ 350	1,000
5	707	150		850
6	708	700		150
7	709	120	2,300	2,330
10	710	340	200 CM #1	2,190
12	711	980		1,210
14			650	1,860
15	712	70		
		100 DM #1		1,690
16		120 DM #2		1,570
18	713	630	500 CM #2	1,440
20	714	170	1,500	2,770
25		40 DM #3		2,730
28	716	260		2,470
31		15 DM #4	10 CM #3	2,465

Debit memoranda:
#1 authorized payment to United Way
#2 return of deposited check from customer
for nonsufficient funds
#3 payment for safety box rental
#4 monthly service charge

Credit memoranda:
#1 collection of note for Tower from third party
#2 wire transfer of funds from foreign bank for revenue
#3 interest earned on checking account balance

4. *Begin with the end-of-month bank balance.*
Bank balance as of May 31 $2,465

5. <u>Add</u>:
cash on hand   50   (May 10)

<u>Add</u>:
deposit in transit   <u>800</u>   <u>850</u>   (May 31)
    Subtotal $3,315

6. <u>Deduct</u>:
checks outstanding   <u>510</u>   (check #715)

(7. There are no bank errors.)
Adjusted bank balance   <u>$2,805</u>

Now that you have adjusted the bank balance, you are ready to reconcile the Cash account.

Part II: Adjusting Tower's Cash Ledger Account

8. Begin with the end-of-month ledger Cash account balance.
Book balance
    as of May 31 $2,370

9. <u>Add</u>:
note collection   200
   (credit memorandum #1, May 10)

<u>Add</u>:
wire transfer   500
   (credit memorandum #2, May 18

<u>Add</u>:
interest income   <u>+ 10</u>   <u>710</u>
   (credit memorandum #3, May 31)
     Subtotal balance $3,080

10. <u>Deduct</u>:
United Way payment   100
   (debit memorandum #1, May 15)

<u>Deduct</u>: NSF check (debit memorandum #2, May 16)	120	
<u>Deduct</u>: safe-deposit rental (debit memorandum #3, May 25)	40	
<u>Deduct</u>: bank service charge (debit memorandum #4, May 31)	<u>15</u>	<u>275</u>

(11. There are no book errors.)
Adjusted Cash balance $2,805

12. Record in the general journal the journal entries for each adjustment to Cash and for any book errors.

For Tower, the following entries must be made (see the "Debit memoranda" and "Credit memoranda" explanations at the bottom of Tower's bank statement):

Cash	200	
Note Receivable		200
To record note collected by bank from Simpson Co.		

Cash	500	
Revenue		500
To record bank wire transfer of revenue from foreign bank		

Cash	10	
Interest Income		10
To record interest on bank account average balance		

Donation Expense	100	
Cash		100
To record automatic deduction for United Way		

Accounts Receivable,	120	
Cash		120
To record NSF check of returned by bank		

Miscellaneous Expense	40	
Cash		40

To record 6 months' rental fee for safe-deposit box

Miscellaneous Expense	15	
Cash		15

To record bank service charge

Of course, it saves time to record these entries as a single compound entry:

Cash	435*	
Donation	100	
Miscellaneous Expense	55	
Accounts Receivable	120	
Note Receivable		200
Interest Income		10
Revenue		500

To record items from May 31 bank reconciliation

*Total debits to Cash − total credits to Cash in the individual entries above.

13. *Notify the bank of any bank errors.* There are no errors in Tower's bank statement.

You have now completed the bank reconciliation and adjusted Tom's books.

Bank Reconciliation Example 2: Reconciling the Cash account and bank statement when there are errors

The Farrell Company started business on August 1, and opened a checking account with a $5,000 deposit. On August 31, it sent in a deposit for $500. There is one check outstanding for $50. (See Figure 2-2, page 22).

Part I: Adjusting Farrell's Bank Balance

1. *If the bank has returned cancelled checks, put them in numerical order.* Assume this has been done.

2. *Examine each canceled check.* You verify that each Farrell check is properly signed and that the amount on the check and on the bank

Figure 2-2
Bank Statement Data

Date	Check no.	Checks and other withdrawals	Deposits and other additions	Balance
1			$5,000	$5,000
4	#1	425	1,200	5,775
8	#2	2,650		3,125
10	#3	613	300	2,812
15			750	3,562
18	#4	37	100	3,625
19	#5	2,075		1,550
22	#1040	200	75	1,425
24			300	1,725
28			95	1,820
31		20 DM #1		1,800

Debit memoranda:
#1 Corporate account fee: August

Farrell Company Cash Account Data for the Month Ended August 31

	Cash receipts		Cash disbursements	
		Balance	**Check no.**	
August 1		$5,000	#1	$ 425
2	$1,200		#2	2,650
8	300		#3	613
13	750		#4	37
15	100		#5	2,075
16	95			
20	75		#6	50
28	500			
		3,020		
		$8,020		$5,850
August 31 balance		$2,170		

statement is the same as the amount in the Cash account. This reveals that check #6 for $50 has not yet cleared. It also reveals that check #1040 for $200 is for the *Harrell* Company—clearly a bank error. You set aside this check.

3. *Verify that the deposit amounts listed on the bank statement conform to the deposit amounts on Farrell's deposit slips (not shown) and the deposits listed in Farrell's Cash account.* You note that the bank has recorded a $300 deposit on August 24 for which there is no corresponding entry in the ledger Cash account. You also note that $500 recorded on the books and deposited in the bank on August 28 does not appear on the bank statement.

4. *Begin with the end-of-month bank balance.*
Bank balance as of August 31 $1,800

5. Add:
deposit in transit   500
                                                      $2,300

6. Deduct:
check outstanding   50
   (check #6)
                                                      $2,250

7. Add:
amount of check incorrectly
   charged to Farrell   200
   Adjusted bank balance $2,450

Part II: Adjusting Farrell's Cash Ledger Account

8. *Begin with the end-of-month ledger Cash account balance.*
Book balance as of August 31 $2,170

9. Add: (there are no additions)

10. Deduct:
bank service charge   20
Adjusted book balance $2,150

There is a problem: the adjusted Cash balance is $300 less than the adjusted bank balance of $2,450, so the amounts are not yet reconciled. Before continuing, try to find the problem.

The problem is that the $300 deposit recorded by the bank on August 24 was never recorded in Cash. You determine that this amount was revenue. When this book error is added back, the Cash account and bank balance are reconciled (they are equal).

Book balance as of August 31	$2,170

9. <u>Add</u>: (There are no additions)

10. <u>Deduct</u>:

bank service charge	20
	$2,150

11. <u>Add</u>:

book error)	300
Adjusted Cash balance	$2,450

12. ***Record in the general journal the journal entries for each adjustment to Cash and for any book errors.***

Cash	300	
Revenue		300
To record bank deposit of 8/24 not recorded in Cash		

Miscellaneous Expense	20	
Cash		20
To record bank service charge		

13. *Notify the bank of any bank errors.* Notify the bank of the Harrell check mistakenly drawn on the Farrell account and return the check immediately.

Farrell's bank reconciliation and the resulting required adjustments to its books are now complete.

Important: The bank reconciliation is more than just a check for accuracy. When a bank or other creditor inquires about company assets, usually the Cash account cannot be reported as an asset until the Cash account has been reconciled with the bank statement.

Summary

The company bank and ledger Cash accounts rarely show the same balance at the end of a period. The disparity is caused by timing differences such as deposits made by the company not on the current bank statement, company disbursements (checks) not yet cleared by the bank and safe-deposit or other bank fees not yet recorded in Cash. The bank reconciliation brings the book and bank accounts into balance and may reveal bank and/or book errors. The company never needs to record adjusting entries for adjustments to the bank balance, but may need to record them for adjustments to the book balance.

QUIZ 1   THE BANK RECONCILIATION

Problem I.

Multiple choice. Circle the correct answer.

1. To find the correct bank statement cash balance for a reconciliation:

    a. deduct from the end-of-month bank balance all checks outstanding
    b. deduct from the end-of-month bank balance only those checks outstanding that were written in the current period
    c. deduct from the end-of-month bank balance checks outstanding that were written in the current period and add checks outstanding that were written in previous periods
    d. add to the end-of-month bank balance all checks outstanding

2. Which of these will make the bank balance lower than the book balance?

    a. a payment your company authorized the bank to make to a third party and which your company has not recorded
    b. a NSF check
    c. a deposit in transit
    d. all of the above

3. The bank statement balance of $7,000 does not include a check outstanding of $1,000, a deposit in transit of $325, but does include a bank service charge of $25 and another company's $100 check erroneously charged against your firm's account (not recorded in the Cash account). The reconciled bank balance is:

    a. $6,400   b. $6,575   c. $6,425   d. $6,625

4. You issued a check for $457 but recorded it at $475. In your bank reconciliation, you will:

    a. Add $18 to the end-of-month bank balance
    b. Add $18 to the end-of-month book balance
    c. Deduct $18 from the end-of-month bank balance
    d. Deduct $18 from the end-of-month book balance

5. If you find another company's canceled check for $450 recorded on your bank statement, you correct the error by:

    a. adding $450 to the end-of-month bank balance
    b. adding $450 to the end-of-month Cash balance
    c. deducting $450 from the end-of-month bank balance
    d. deducting $450 from the end-of-month Cash balance

Problem II.

Fill in the blanks.

1. Cash deposits in the company checking account are a _____ _____ to the company bank statement, but a _____ to the company ledger Cash account.

2. A bank _____ memorandum shows an amount added by the bank to the company checking account; a bank _____ memorandum shows an amount subtracted by the bank from the company checking account.

3. To reconcile the monthly bank balance, a $630 check outstanding is _____ _____ the current bank balance.

4. When a bank or creditor inquires about company finances, the ledger Cash account usually cannot be reported as a(n) _____ until it has been reconciled.

Problem III.

What are the three primary goals of a bank reconciliation?

1. _____

2. _____

3. _____

Problem IV.

You are doing a bank reconciliation with the following balances:

Bank statement June 30 balance		$x,xxx
Additions	_____	
Deductions	_____	
Adjusted June 30 bank balance		$x,xxx
Company Cash account		
June 30 balance		$x,xxx
Additions	_____	
Deductions	_____	
Adjusted June 30 Cash balance		$x,xxx

Numbers 1–5 describe the action to take with items in the bank reconciliation:

1—Add to the end-of-month bank balance

2—Deduct from the end-of-month bank balance

3—Add to the end-of-month Cash balance

4—Deduct from the end-of-month Cash balance

5—No action required

For each item and event below, insert the number of the appropriate action.

Example: <u>5</u> Check #107, which is not on the bank statement, was cancelled because it was written for the wrong amount. Assume that the Cash account was properly corrected.

Here are the items and events:

a. On July 2, you receive a letter from the bank saying that it collected a note for the company on June 29.
b. Two checks written in June had not cleared the bank as of June 30.
c. Another firm's check was included with the company's June 30 bank statement and deducted on the bank account.
d. A May deposit in transit was recorded on the June 30 bank statement.
e. A company deposit was mailed on June 30 and received by the bank on July 1.
f. A memo was included with the June 30 bank statement charging the company for printing its checks.
g. You discovered that a cash receipt entered in the company journal was never posted to Cash.

Problem V.

Davis Company's June bank reconciliation includes the following data:

a. June 30 end-of-month bank statement balance: $7,000.
b. June 30 end-of-month Cash account balance: $6,250.
c. May 31 deposit in transit recorded on the June bank statement: $700.
d. June 30 deposit in transit: $500.
e. May 31 check outstanding deducted on the June bank statement: $450.
f. May 31 outstanding checks not deducted on the June bank statement: $150.
g. Checks issued by Davis in June but outstanding as of June 30: $800.
h. Service charge recorded on the June bank statement: $40.
i. Interest earned on checking account average balance per June bank statement: $15
j. NSF check from G. Slack Co.: $320.
k. Note collected by bank for Davis and recorded on the bank statement: $600.
l. Canceled check for $205 was credited to Cash as $250.

1. Prepare Davis's June bank reconciliation.

2. Give all required journal entries to correct any errors.

QUIZ 1   *Solutions and Explanations*

Problem I.

1. a

2. d

3. c

$7,000 end-of-month bank balance + $325 deposit in transit – $1,000 checks outstanding + $100 for check erroneously charged to your firm's account = $6,425 reconciled bank balance. The $25 bank service charge deducted to adjust the Cash account is not used to adjust the bank balance.

4. b

5. a

Problem II.

1. credit; debit

2. credit; debit

3. deducted from

4. asset

Problem III.

1. To review information needed to bring company accounting records up to date at the end of the month or other period;

2. to verify that the ledger Cash account balance at the end of the month or other period is accurate and to correct any errors; and

3. to verify that the checking account balance at the end of the month or other period is accurate and to alert the bank of any errors.

Problem IV.

a. 3
Add to the end-of-month Cash balance.

b. 2
Deduct from the end-of-month bank balance.

c. 1
Add to the end-of-month bank balance.

d. 5
No action required; this was added in the May bank reconciliation.

e. 1
Add to the end-of-month bank balance.

f. 4
Deduct from the end-of-month Cash balance.

g. 3
Add to the end-of-month Cash balance.

Problem V.

1. The Davis company June bank reconciliation is as follows:

Bank balance as of June 30		$7,000
<u>Add</u>: June deposit in transit		<u>500</u>
		7,500
<u>Deduct:</u>		
May outstanding checks	150	
June outstanding checks	<u>800</u>	<u>950</u>
Adjusted June 30 bank balance		$6,550
Book balance as of June 30		$6,250
<u>Add:</u>		
interest income	15	
note collection	<u>600</u>	
		<u>615</u>
		6,865
<u>Deduct:</u>		
service charge	40	
NSF check	<u>320</u>	<u>360</u>
		6,505
<u>Add:</u>		
error correction		<u>45</u>
Adjusted June 30 book balance		$6,550

Note for c: The May 31 $700 deposit in transit was added to Davis's May end-of-month bank balance when the May reconciliation was performed. Because the June bank statement now shows the transaction, the temporary timing difference has been eliminated.

Note for f: Similarly, no action is required on the May 31 outstanding checks of $450 because they were deducted from the June bank balance. Now that they have been paid, the temporary timing difference has been eliminated.

Note for l: The $45 added back is for the transposition: this credit to Cash should have been for $205 but was transposed to $250.

2. Davis Company must make the following journal entries:

Cash	15	
Interest Income		15
To record interest on average bank account balance		

Cash	600	
Note Receivable		600
To record note collected by bank from Simpson Co.		

Cash	45	
Accounts Payable		45
To correct error		

Miscellaneous expense	40	
Cash		40
To record bank service charge		

Accounts Receivable, G. Slack	320	
Cash		320
To record NSF check of G. Slack returned by bank		

Or as one compound entry:

Cash	300*	
Miscellaneous Expense	40	
Accounts Receivable	320	
Interest Income		15
Note Receivable		600
Accounts Payable		45
To record items from bank reconciliation		

* $660 total debits – $360 total credits = $300 debit to Cash (to balance)

QUIZ 2   THE BANK RECONCILIATION

Problem I.

Multiple choice. Circle the correct answer.

1. When reconciling the Cash account, direct deposits such as wire transfers are:

   a. deducted from the Cash balance
   b. added to the Cash balance
   c. deducted from the bank balance
   d. added to the bank balance

2. In a bank reconciliation, which of the following items are added to the end-of-month ledger Cash account balance?

   a. outstanding checks
   b. interest earned on average checking account balance
   c. deposits in transit from the month covered by the bank statement
   d. none of the above

3. A canceled check written for $110 is enclosed in your company's bank statement, but the statement shows that the check cleared for $100. When you do the bank reconciliation, you should . . .

   a. add $10 to the bank balance
   b. add $10 to the ledger Cash account balance
   c. subtract $10 from the ledger Cash account balance
   d. subtract $10 from the bank balance

Problem II.

Fill in the blanks.

1. A company check is a _____ to Cash, but is a _____ on the bank statement.

2. Upon completion of a bank reconciliation, the company records adjustments to the ledger _____ account.

3. When the bank returns a NSF check, it issues a _____ (debit/ credit) memorandum that appears on the company bank statement; the company must then _____ (debit/credit) the ledger Cash account for the amount of the NSF check.

Problem III.

Define the following terms.

    a. Deposits in transit
    b. Outstanding checks
    c. NSF check
    d. Reconciled Cash balance

Problem IV.

You are given the following bank statement and Cash account transactions and items for the bank reconciliation.

Bank statement April 30 balance	$x,xxx
Additions	_____
Deductions	_____
Adjusted April 30 cash balance	$x,xxx

Company Cash account	
April 30 balance	$x,xxx
Additions	_____
Deductions	_____
Adjusted April 30 cash balance	$x,xxx

    a. There is company cash on hand.
    b. A deposit was mailed on April 30 and received by the bank on May 1.
    c. Checks written in March have not cleared the bank as of April 30.
    d. Checks drawn in April have not cleared the bank as of April 30.
    e. A credit memorandum was issued for a bank error the company reported in March.
    f. An April 30 credit memorandum was issued for a wire transfer of foreign funds.
    g. The company misposted an $800 deposit to Cash as a debit of $80.

For each item above, insert the number of the appropriate action.

1—Add to the end-of-month bank balance

2—Deduct from the end-of-month bank balance

3—Add to the end-of-month Cash balance

4—Deduct from the end-of-month Cash balance

5—No action required

Problem V.

Marvel, Inc.'s May bank reconciliation includes the following data:

  a. May 31 end-of-month bank balance: $5,360.
  b. May 31 Marvel end-of-month Cash account balance: $4,880.
  c. April 30 deposit in transit recorded on the May bank statement: $300.
  d. May 31 deposit in transit: $200.
  e. April 30 checks outstanding deducted on the May bank statement: $260.
  f. April 30 checks outstanding not deducted on the May bank statement: $75.
  g. Checks issued by Marvel in May but outstanding as of May 31: $275.
  h. Service charge recorded on the May bank statement: $30.
  i. Marvel cash on hand (undeposited cash): $80.
  j. Automatic payment on a note payable to Bryan Co. recorded on the May bank statement but not recorded by Marvel: $500.
  k. Customer had placed an order which your firm refused to process until it got the cash. May bank statement includes a wire transfer: $1,000.
  l. Another company's check was deducted from Marvel's May bank statement: $60.

1. Prepare Marvel's May bank reconciliation.

2. Give all required journal entries based on the bank reconciliation.

QUIZ 2   *Solutions and Explanations*

Problem I.

1. b

2. b

3. d

Problem II.

1. credit; debit

2. Cash

3. debit memorandum; credit

Problem III.

a. *Deposits in transit* are deposits made by the company but not yet recorded by the bank.

b. *Outstanding checks* are checks written, recorded and disbursed by the company but not yet paid by the bank.

c. A *NSF check* is a check returned by the bank for "not sufficient funds."

d. The *reconciled Cash balance* is the Cash balance that should be reported on the balance sheet as an asset of the company, i.e., the correct Cash balance.

Problem IV.

a. 1

Add to the end-of-month bank balance.

b. 1

Add to the end-of-month bank balance.

c. 2

Deduct from the end-of-month bank balance.

d. 2

Deduct from the end-of-month bank balance.

e. 5

No action required; this was added to the bank statement balance in the March reconciliation.

f. 3

Add to the end-of-month Cash balance.

g. 3

Add ($720) to the end-of-month Cash balance ($800 correct amount − $80 already entered = $720 entered to make correct amount).

Problem V.

1. Marvel's May bank reconciliation is as follows:

Bank balance as of May 31		$5,360
Add:		
Cash on hand (undeposited)	$ 80	
May deposit in transit	200	280
		5,640
Deduct:		
April outstanding checks	75	
May outstanding checks	275	350
Interim May 31 balance		$5,290
Add:		
bank error		60
Adjusted May 31 bank balance		$5,350
Book balance as of May 31		$4,880
Add:		
wire transfer		1,000
		5,880
Deduct:		
bank service charge	30	
automatic payment	500	530
Adjusted May 31 book balance		$5,350

Note for c: The April 30 deposit in transit of $300 was added to the bank balance in the April reconciliation. With its appearance on the actual May statement, the timing difference is now eliminated.

Note for e: The April 30 outstanding check of $260 was deducted from the bank balance in the April reconciliation. With its appearance on the May statement, the timing difference is now eliminated.

2. Marvel must make the following journal entries:

Cash	1,000	
Sales Revenue		1,000

To record wire transfer

Miscellaneous Expense	30	
Cash		30

To record bank service charge

Note Payable	500	
Cash		500

To record automatic payment on note due to Bryan Co.

Or as one compound entry:

Cash	470*	
Miscellaneous Expense	30	
Note Payable, Bryan	500	
Revenue		1,000

To record items from May 31 bank reconciliation

* $1,000 debit to Cash – $30 credit to Cash – $500 credit to Cash = $470 total debit to Cash.

No adjusting entry is necessary for cash on hand because it is already recorded in the Cash account.

FINDING AND CORRECTING ERRORS USING THE UNADJUSTED TRIAL BALANCE

The trial balance is an ordered listing of all ledger accounts and their balances. It may be taken (produced) at any time. If the account has a *debit* balance, list the balance in the left column; If the account has a *credit* balance, list it in the right column. If total debits do not equal total credits, a mistake has been made. Total debits and credits are also known as *hash totals* because they have no purpose in accounting other than to reveal errors.

There are three kinds of trial balances and they are produced sequentially: unadjusted, adjusted followed by the post closing. Only the unadjusted trial balance is used in this section unless otherwise noted.

Some errors described in this section are found only in manual accounting systems, but knowledgeable accounting professionals should be able to handle accounting errors that may occur in manual or computerized systems.

Normal Account Balances

An account's *normal balance* is the side on which an *increase* is recorded. Some accounts have a normal debit balance; others, a normal credit balance.

1. **Balance sheet accounts**. Balance sheet accounts include assets, liabilities and owners' equity and have the following normal balances:

- *Asset accounts have a normal debit balance (a debit to an asset account increases it)*. Examples: Cash, Accounts Receivable, Equipment.

- *Liability accounts have a normal credit balance (a credit to a liability account increases it)*. Examples: Accounts Payable, Mortgage Payable.

- *Owners' equity accounts have a normal credit balance (a credit to an owners' equity account increases it)*. Examples: corporation accounts such as Capital Stock and Retained Earnings; sole proprietorship or partnership accounts such as Owners' Capital.

The easiest way to remember normal account balances is to use the accounting equation: Assets = Liabilities + Owners' Equity. Accounts on the left side of the equation (assets) have a normal debit balance; accounts on the right side of the equation (liabilities and owners' equity) have a normal credit balance.

2. **Income statement accounts.** Income statement accounts include revenue and expense accounts.

- *Revenue accounts have a normal credit balance (a credit to a revenue account increases it).* Revenue accounts increase income.

- *Expense accounts have a normal debit balance (a debit to an expense account increases it).* Expense accounts decrease income.

Contra Accounts

A *contra account* is directly related to a specific asset, liability or stockholders' (owners') equity, revenue or expense account. The contra account has the opposite normal balance of its related account.

1. **Balance sheet contra accounts.** Typical examples of balance sheet contra accounts follow:

- *Asset contra accounts.* Accounts Receivable has a debit balance; its contra account, Allowance for Doubtful Accounts, has a credit balance. Equipment has a debit balance; its contra account, Accumulated Depreciation—Equipment, has a credit balance.

- *Liability contra accounts.* Bonds Payable has a credit balance; its contra account, Discount on Bonds Payable, has a debit balance.

2. **Income statement contra accounts.** Income statement accounts also have their contra accounts:

- *Owners' equity contra accounts.* Most owners' equity accounts have a normal credit balance, but Treasury Stock has a debit balance and is treated as a contra account to total Owners' Equity (rather than to a particular account). Dividends Declared has a debit balance and is a contra account to Retained Earnings.

- *Revenue contra accounts.* Sales has a credit balance; its contra accounts, Sales Discounts and Sales Returns and Allowances, have debit balances.

- *Expense contra accounts.* Purchases has a debit balance; its contra accounts, Purchase Discounts and Purchase Returns and Allowances, have credit balances.

When Correct Account Balances May Not Be Normal

Generally, an account balance that is not normal is incorrect, but there are exceptions. For example, if a company overdraws its bank account, the Cash account (normal debit balance) will have a temporary credit balance. Similarly, if bills are overpaid, Accounts Payable (normal credit balance) may have a temporary debit balance. If a company is operating at a loss, Retained Earnings (credit balance) may have a debit balance.

Locating Trial Balance Errors Step by Step

To find errors causing the trial balance to be out of balance, you will go through the accounting cycle in reverse, as follows:

A. Make sure the account balances were correctly transferred to the trial balance. Work *from the general ledger to the trial balance*, to see that:

- no ledger account debit balance appears in the credit column or vice versa—use Figure 3-1 (page 44) as a reference to see which account balances go in each column;

- each account balance matches the one on the trial balance; and

- every ledger account that has a balance is on the trial balance.

If no errors are found, or errors are found and corrected, and the trial balance does not balance, go to step B.

Figure 3-1
Normal Balances of Various Ledger Accounts

Account	Normal Balance	
Asset accounts		
Cash	Debit balance	
(Various titles) Receivable	Debit balance	
Allowance for Doubtful Accounts		Credit balance
Inventory	Debit balance	
Prepaid (Various titles)	Debit balance	
Land	Debit balance	
Building	Debit balance	
Equipment	Debit balance	
Accumulated Depreciation—(Various titles)		Credit balance
Liability accounts		
(Various titles) Payable		Credit balance
Discount on Bonds Payable	Debit balance	
(Various titles) Revenue in Advance		Credit balance
or Unearned (Various titles) Revenue		Credit balance
Owners' equity accounts		
Capital (Common and/or Preferred) Stock*		Credit balance
Retained Earnings*		Credit balance
Dividends Declared**	Debit balance	
Treasury Stock	Debit balance	
Revenue accounts		
(Various titles) Revenue		Credit balance
Sales Returns and Allowances	Debit balance	
Expense accounts		
Purchases	Debit balance	
Freight-In	Debit balance	
Purchase Discounts		Credit balance
Purchase Returns and Allowances		Credit balance
Cost of Goods Sold	Debit balance	
(Various titles) Expense	Debit balance	
(Various titles) Loss	Debit balance	
(Various titles) Gain		Credit balance

* If the entity is a partnership or sole proprietorship, the account Owner's Capital (normal credit balance) is used and it appears on the statement of capital.

** If the entity is a partnership or sole proprietorship, the account Withdrawal is used; this account appears on the statement of capital.

B. See if the ledger account balances have been calculated correctly.

If no errors are found, or errors are found and corrected, and the trial balance still does not balance, go to step C.

C. Check the journal entries and postings for errors, as follows:

1. Work *from the journal to the ledger* to see that journal entries were posted correctly.

2. Review journal entries for obvious errors, such as unequal debits and credits. If you find a discrepancy, you may have to go to the source documents to make corrections.

If no errors are found, or errors are found and corrected, and the trial balance still does not balance, return to step A and repeat the process.

How the Steps Work in Detail

A. Check that account balances have been correctly transferred to the trial balance.

Obvious errors can be found simply by eyeballing the trial balance to see if amounts are in the correct column based on whether they normally have a debit or credit balance. To spot a mistake when an account does not have a normal balance requires more than eyeballing, which will be discussed later.

You can "eyeball" a trial balance for the following errors:

Doubling errors. If the *only* error in the trial balance is just one account balance in the wrong column, find it as follows: Find the difference between the debit and credit column totals. This amount is *double* the amount of the error, so divide it by 2 to yield the amount of the account balance that is out of place.

Slide Error. If an account has an *unreasonable* balance, the error may be a slide. A *slide* error occurs when one or more zeros are added to or deleted from an amount—such as 1,650 written as 16,500 (zero added) or as 165 (zero deleted). Another example: 2,036 written as 236 (zero deleted) or as 200,036 (two zeros added).

For example, a balance in Property, Plant and Equipment of $1,000 may be unreasonably low and therefore may be a slide error (because it is more likely to have a balance of $10,000 or $100,000). Similarly, a balance in Office Supplies Expense of $15,000 may be unreasonably high due to a slide error (because it is much more likely to have a balance of $1,500 or $150).

If the difference between total debits and total credits is exactly divisible by 9 and there is only one error causing the problem, the error may be a slide, as explained above, or a *transposition*, which occurs as follows:

Transposition Error. A *transposition* error occurs when two digits are reversed, such as 920 written as 290. If the difference between the debit and credit column totals is exactly divisible by 9 and there is only one error causing the problem, that error may be a transposition or slide. To find a transposition, follow these steps:

Step a. Find the difference between total debits and credits, add 1 to the first digit of the difference and you have an amount we will call X. You will now investigate every ledger account balance where the difference between the first and second digits of the balance is X.

For example, assume that the difference between total debits and credits is $540: 5 (first digit of 540) + 1 = 6. You will investigate every ledger account balance where the difference between the first and second digits is exactly 6.

The following example shows how to tell if there is a transposition error. For purposes of illustration, a partial trial balance is shown using account balances without the account titles.

ABC Company's Trial Balance

Debit	Credit
$ 911	
585	
703	
1,210	
	$ 255
	277
	1,812
	719
514	
	745
	857
472	
$4,395	$4,665

There is a difference between total debits and credits of $270 ($4,395 debits − $4,665 credits = − $270) and it is divisible by 9 (270/9 = 30).

To see if the difference of 270 may be the result of a transposition error, add 1 to the first digit of the difference: 2 (first digit of 270) + 1 = 3. Investigate all account balances where the difference between the first and second digits is exactly 3:

Starting from the top of the trial balance:

First debit balance: 911. 9 (first digit) − 1 (second digit) = 8. Do not investigate.

Second debit balance: 585. 5 (first digit) − 8 (second digit) = 3. Investigate.

Third debit balance: 703. 7 (first digit) − 0 (second digit) = 7. Do not investigate.

Fourth debit balance: 1,210. 1 (first digit) − 2 (second digit) = 1. Do not investigate.

<u>Fifth debit balance</u>: 514. 5 (first digit) – 1 (second digit) = 4. Do not investigate.

<u>Sixth debit balance</u>: 472. 4 (first digit) – 7 (second digit) = 3. Investigate.

After checking all balances, you conclude that you must investigate the debit balances of 585 and 472, and the credit balances of 255, 745, and 857.

EXAMPLE 1: Here is a partial trial balance for RenCo. For teaching purposes, account balances are shown without account titles.

Debit	Credit
$ 725	
620	
	$ 115
	520
	480
160	
795	
	737
	808
$2,300	$2,660

$2,660 total credits – $2,300 total debits = $360 difference. Is the difference divisible by 9? 360/9 = 40. Yes, so the error is probably a transposition or slide. You found no slide error, so you must check for a transposition.

3 (first digit of $360) + 1 = 4. Investigate all account balances where the difference between the first and second digits is 4.

Step b. See if correcting the error will increase (**I**) or decrease (**D**) the debit or credit total.

Total debits	Total credits
$2,300	$2,660

There are three accounts that must be investigated: a debit balance of $620 (6 – 2 = 4), and two credit balances of $480 (8 – 4 = 4) and $737 (7 – 3 = 4).

Debit balance:

$620   620 – 260 = 360 **D**

If $620 is a transposition of $260, correcting it will decrease total debits by $360, so it is marked with a **D**. This account cannot be the cause of the error because total debits are already less than total credits, and decreasing total debits would only enlarge the error. You move on to the credit balances.

Credit balances:

$480	840 – 480 = 360	**I**
$737	773 – 737 = 36	**I**
or	737 – 377 = 360	**D**

If $480 is a transposition of $840, correcting it will *increase* total credits, so it is marked with an **I**. This account cannot be the cause of the problem because total credits are already more than total debits (increasing total credits would enlarge the error).

If $737 is a transposition of $773, correcting it will *increase* total credits, so it is marked with an **I**. This account cannot be the cause of the problem because the difference is only 36, not 360.

If $737 is a transposition of $377, correcting it will *decrease* total credits by $360. To compute: $2,660 total credits – $360 = $2,300. Because total debits are $2,300, the transposition may be what is causing the problem.

When the first digit of the imbalance is 9:

If you add 9 + 1 you get 10, but you cannot have a difference of 10 between two digits, so the number 1 is used. Thus, if the difference between total debits is, say, 927, investigate any account balance with a difference between the first and second digits of 1.

EXAMPLE 2: You are reviewing the account balances from a partial trial balance that contains an error.

Debit	Credit
$ 1,100	
1,700	
	$ 850
2,400	
	680
1,300	
7,400	
	3,800
	2,590
	230
	4,000
	10,000
640	
	100
7,000	
210	
590	
$22,340	$22,250

$22,340 total debits – $22,250 total credits = $90 difference. 9 (first digit of difference) + 1 = 10. You will investigate each account with a difference between the first two digits of 1. Assume that you have narrowed your investigation to accounts with a balance of $210 and $230.

Debit balance:

$210   210 – 120 = 90 **D**

If $210 is a transposition, correcting it will decrease total debits, so it is marked with a **D**. This account may be the source of the problem.

Credit balance:

$230   320 − 230 = 90 **I**

If $230 is a transposition, correcting it will increase total credits, so it is marked with an **I**. This account may be the cause of the problem.

Either account may be causing the difference, so both should be investigated.

Important: Transpositions and slides can occur at any point in accounting, including the bank reconciliation (Section 2). Any time an error is exactly divisible by 9, look for two digits reversed or an added or deleted "0."

If the error is not due to doubling, a transposition or slide, look for errors that occurred when account balances were transferred from the ledger to the trial balance.

To do this, you must follow the steps described at the beginning of this section in more detail, as follows:

A. Make sure the account balances were correctly transferred to the trial balance. *Work from the general ledger to the trial balance* to see that:

- no ledger account debit balance appears in the credit column on the trial balance or vice versa;

- each account balance matches the one on the trial balance; and

- every ledger account that has a balance is on the trial balance.

If no errors are found, or errors are found and corrected, and the trial balance does not balance, go to step B.

B. See if the ledger account balances have been calculated correctly.

Review the accuracy of the ledger account balances. If you posted the journal entries to the accounts, you almost always know which account is likely to contain an error.

The following Cash account has a debit balance of $700. Is it correct?

Cash

Debit	Credit
900	300
500	200
600	700
Bal. 700	

No, it is not correct. The correct debit balance is $800, not $700. To calculate: $2,000 total debits (900 + 500 + 600) – $1,200 total credits (300 + 200 + 700) = $800.

Transferring the incorrect debit balance of $700 will make total debits on the trial balance $100 less than total credits.

If no errors are found, or if after correcting errors that are found, the trial balance still does not balance, go to step C.

C. Check the journal entries and postings for errors, as follows.

1. Work *from the journal to the ledger* to see that journal entries were posted correctly.

For example, when the following journal entry to record a cash sale . . .

| Accounts Receivable | 300 | |
| Sales | | 300 |

. . . was posted to Accounts Receivable, it was recorded as a credit:

Accounts Receivable

Debit	Credit
	300

This mistake will cause a $600 error in the trial balance—total debits will be $300 too low and total credits will be $300 too high (another example of a "doubling" error).

Or, only part of a correct journal entry may be posted to the ledger. For example, say when the following entry . . .

Utility Expense	75	
Cash		75

. . . was debited to Utility Expense, it was never credited to Cash. This error would cause total debits on the trial balance to be $75 more than total credits. Or, the wrong amount may have been posted. For example, say that the journal entry . . .

Accounts Receivable	200	
Sales		200

. . . was posted as:

Sales

Debit	Credit
	500

This would result in total credits on the trial balance being $300 ($500 – $200) more than total debits.

2. Review journal entries for obvious errors, such as unequal debits and credits. If you find a journal entry with unequal total debits and credits, you may have to go to the source documents to be sure amounts are corrected properly.

For example, assume that the following journal entry was posted to the accounts.

Cash	300	
Sales Revenue		800

When the balances in Cash and Sales Revenue are transferred to the trial balance, total credits will be $500 more than total debits. Because there is an error, proceed to step E.

If no errors are found, or if after correcting errors that are found, the trial balance still does not balance, you have overlooked one or more errors and should return to step A and repeat the process.

Trial Balance Error Detection— A Case Example

Exhibit 3-1 on page 55 (make a copy if needed) is an unadjusted trial balance that is out of balance—total credits are greater than total debits. Assume that both column totals have been added correctly.

A. Check that account balances have been correctly transferred to the trial balance.

You eyeball the trial balance as described earlier:

- The $200 balance for Allowance for Doubtful Accounts, a contra account to Accounts Receivable, is properly listed in the credit column.

- The $40,000 balance for Investments, an asset (debit balance), is incorrectly listed in the credit column. Transfer the $40,000 to the debit column.

- The Accumulated Depreciation—Buildings balance of $70,000 is correctly listed in the credit column; it is a contra account to Buildings (normal debit balance). But Accumulated Depreciation—Equipment, another contra account to Equipment, should have its $36,000 balance in the credit column, not in the debit column as shown. Transfer the $36,000 balance to the credit column.

- Liability and owners' equity accounts (from Accounts Payable through Retained Earnings) have credit balances. Property Taxes Payable has a $500 balance incorrectly listed as a debit (liabilities have a credit balance). Transfer the $500 to the credit column. (If this were your company, you would check to see if this is a tax rebate—a receivable, which should have a debit balance. If it is a tax rebate, you would leave it in the debit column.)

- Unamortized Discount on Bonds Payable, a contra account to Bonds Payable, has a $4,000 balance correctly listed in the debit column. As a contra account to Bonds Payable, a liability account with a credit balance, Unamortized Discount on Bonds Payable has a debit balance.

- Two sales account balances appear in the debit column: Sales Discounts, a contra account to Sales, with a $7,000 balance correctly

Exhibit 3-1
XYZ Company's Trial Balance

	Debits	Credits
Cash	$ 60,200	
Accounts Receivable	48,000	
Allowance for Doubtful Accounts		$ 200
Inventory	110,000	
Office Supplies	900	
Prepaid Inurance	500	
Long-Term Note Receivable	12,000	
Investments		40,000
Land	60,000	
Equipment	182,300	
Accumulated Depreciation–Equipment	36,000	
Buildings	392,400	
Accumulated Depreciation–Buildings		70,000
Patent, net	28,400	
Accounts Payable		23,000
Notes Payable		5,000
Interest Payable		200
Property Taxes Payable	500	
Bonds Payable		200,000
Unamortized Discount on Bonds Payable	4,000	
Mortgage Payable		50,000
Capital Stock		100,000
Additional Contributed Capital		250,000
Retained Earnings		85,000
Dividends		15,000
Sales Revenue		900,000
Sales Discounts	7,000	
Sales Returns and Allowances	20,000	
Investment Revenue		3,600
Rent Revenue		3,000
Interest Revenue		400
Gain on Sale of Equipment		500
Purchases	455,000	
Purchase Discounts	3,000	
Purchase Returns and Allowances		7,000
Selling Expense	2,000	
Depreciation Expense	1,500	
Salary Expense	250,000	
Administrative Expense	40,000	
Interest Expense	8,000	
Loss on Sale of Investment		200
Totals	$1,721,700	$1,753,100

listed in the debit column, and Sales Returns and Allowances, another contra account to Sales, with a debit balance of $20,000.

- Expense accounts, with debit balances, are listed last. Purchase Returns and Allowances, a contra account to Purchases, has a balance of $7,000 correctly listed in the credit column. But Purchase Discounts, another contra account to Purchases, has a balance of $3,000 incorrectly listed in the debit column. Transfer the $3,000 to the credit column. Loss on Sale of Investment has a $200 balance incorrectly listed as a credit. Losses are always debits. Move the $200 balance to the debit column.

When the balances are corrected, accounting personnel create a new trial balance—see Exhibit 3-2 (page 57). Photocopy if needed.

The new trial balance in Exhibit 3-2 is still out of balance: total credits exceed total debits by $30,000. You decide to test for a possible doubling error. To test: $30,000 total difference/2 = $15,000. If there is now only one error and it is a doubling error, it may have been caused by an account with a $15,000 debit balance being in the credit column.

There is one account with $15,000 credit balance, Dividends. This is a contra account to Retained Earnings (credit balance), and therefore it has a debit balance. The error was missed when balances were checked. Transfer the $15,000 balance to the debit column. Note that this could not have been a slide or transposition error because the difference between total debits and credits is not evenly divisible by 9: 30,000/9 = 3333.3

The corrected trial balance, now in balance, is shown in Exhibit 3-3 (page 58).

Errors Not Revealed by the Trial Balance

Even when totals are in balance, there may be errors. For example:

- *Transactions never recorded on company books.* A $150 credit purchase is not recorded. Because both Purchases (debit balance) and Accounts Payable (credit balance) are both understated by $150, there will be no difference in the totals.

Exhibit 3-2
XYZ Company's Trial Balance

	Debits	Credits
Cash	$ 60,200	
Accounts Receivable	48,000	
Allowance for Doubtful Accounts		$ 200
Inventory	110,000	
Office Supplies	900	
Prepaid Inurance	500	
Long-Term Note Receivable	12,000	
Investments	40,000	
Land	60,000	
Equipment	182,300	
Accumulated Depreciation–Equipment		36,000
Buildings	392,400	
Accumulated Depreciation–Buildings		70,000
Patent, net	28,400	
Accounts Payable		23,000
Notes Payable		5,000
Interest Payable		200
Property Taxes Payable		500
Bonds Payable		200,000
Unabortized Discount on Bonds Payable	4,000	
Mortgage Payable		50,000
Capltal Stock		100,000
Additional Contributed Capital		250,000
Retained Earnings		85,000
Dividends		15,000
Sales Revenue		900,000
Sales Discounts	7,000	
Sales Returns and Allowances	20,000	
Investment Revenue		3,600
Rent Revenue		3,000
Interest Revenue		400
Gain on Sale of Equipment		500
Purchases	455,000	
Purchase Discounts		3,000
Purchase Returns and Allowances		7,000
Selling Expense	2,000	
Depreciation Expense	1,500	
Salary Expense	250,000	
Administrative Expense	40,000	
Interest Expense	8,000	
Loss on Sale of Investment	200	
Totals	$1,722,400	$1,752,400

Exhibit 3-3
XYZ Company's Trial Balance

	Debits	Credits
Cash	$ 60,200	
Accounts Receivable	48,000	
Allowance for Doubtful Accounts		$ 200
Inventory	110,000	
Office Supplies	900	
Prepaid Inurance	500	
Long-Term Note Receivable	12,000	
Investments	40,000	
Land	60,000	
Equipment	182,300	
Accumulated Depreciation–Equipment		36,000
Buildings	392,400	
Accumulated Depreciation–Buildings		70,000
Patent, net	28,400	
Accounts Payable		23,000
Notes Payable		5,000
Interest Payable		200
Property Taxes Payable		500
Bonds Payable		200,000
Unamortized Discount on Bonds Payable	4,000	
Mortgage Payable		50,000
Capital Stock		100,000
Additional Contributed Capital		250,000
Retained Earnings		85,000
Dividends	15,000	
Sales Revenue		900,000
Sales Discounts	7,000	
Sales Returns and Allowances	20,000	
Investment Revenue		3,600
Rent Revenue		3,000
Interest Revenue		400
Gain on Sale of Equipment		500
Purchases	455,000	
Purchase Discounts		3,000
Purchase Returns and Allowances		7,000
Selling Expense	2,000	
Depreciation Expense	1,500	
Salary Expense	250,000	
Administrative Expense	40,000	
Interest Expense	8,000	
Loss on Sale of Investment	200	
Totals	$1,737,400	$1,737,400

- *An incorrect amount recorded in the debit and credit of an entry.*
  For example, a credit sale of $430 is recorded as:

Accounts Receivable	340	
Sales		340

The error will not cause a difference because both Accounts Receivable (debit balance) and Sales (credit balance) are understated by $90.

- *Amount recorded in the wrong account.* For example, a $4,000 computer purchase is debited to Office Supplies instead of Equipment. The trial balance will not reveal the error because the amount will still show up in the debit column and there is no automatic way to know that the wrong account was debited. Equipment (debit balance) is understated by $4,000, but Office Supplies is overstated by the same $4,000, restoring the balance in total debits—and disguising the error.

Handling Corrections to the Trial Balance

Companies that are computerized must make correcting journal entries for all errors. New trial balances can be printed as appropriate.

Companies that do their accounting manually can correct inaccurate postings directly on the trial balance and in the ledger account. The correction in the ledger account should contain a note explaining the error correction. For all errors other than inaccurate postings, a correcting journal entry must be made.

The Adjusted Trial Balance

At the end of the accounting cycle, adjusting journal entries are made and posted to the ledger accounts. Then the adjusted trial balance is prepared. If the adjusted trial balance columns do not balance, follow the same steps used on the unadjusted trial balance to find the error—and add this step:

- If you are not using a worksheet, make sure that all accounts listed in the unadjusted trial balance also appear properly on the adjusted trial balance unless they have been removed as the result of an adjustment. Also, make sure that any new accounts that are required by the adjusting entries have been properly created.

For example, if the unadjusted trial balance listed Trucks, then the adjusted trial balance should list Depreciation Expense. If there is a Notes Payable account on the unadjusted trial balance, then the adjusted trial balance should show Interest Payable and Interest Expense.

Once the adjusted trial balance is complete and free of error, the income statement and balance sheet can be prepared.

The Post-Closing Trial Balance

After the income statement (temporary) accounts are closed out for the period, the post-closing trial balance can be prepared. The purpose of the post-closing trial balance is to assure that the general ledger is in balance. The only ledger accounts that remain open at this point are the balance sheet (permanent) accounts. All temporary accounts (revenue, expense, dividend, and withdrawal accounts) and their contra accounts have been closed out.

To review the post-closing trial balance for errors:

1. Make sure that no temporary accounts (such as revenue and expense accounts) are included. These accounts now have zero balances and therefore should not appear on a post-closing trial balance.

2. See that Retained Earnings has the ending, not the beginning, balance; in other words, that income has been included and dividends have been deducted.

3. Determine if debits equal credits. If not, follow the steps described earlier.

Summary

Many accounting errors show up in the trial balance. When total debits do not equal total credits, the investigation moves backward through the accounting cycle step by step. The same method is used, with minor variations, for errors on the adjusted trial balance and post-closing trial balance.

QUIZ 1   FINDING AND CORRECTING ERRORS USING THE UNADJUSTED TRIAL BALANCE

Problem I.

Multiple choice. Circle the correct answer.

1. Which of the following is *not* correct?

    a. A trial balance can be taken at any time.

    b. A trial balance calculates the total assets of a company at a particular time and the net income of a company over a specified period of time.

    c. All accounts with a balance are included on the trial balance.

    d. A trial balance is usually prepared before the financial statements.

2. Asset accounts . . .

    a. have a debit balance

    b. have a credit balance

    c. may have a debit or a credit balance

    d. appear only on the unadjusted trial balance

3. A $120,000 difference in trial balance totals may be caused by:

    a. the Accumulated Depreciation balance of $60,000 being listed as a debit

    b. the Accumulated Depreciation balance of $60,000 being listed as a credit

    c. the Purchases balance being listed as a $60,000 debit

    d. the Purchases balance being listed as a $120,000 debit

4. You discover a $900 difference in your trial balance totals. You have narrowed your investigation to the following account balances. Which one(s) may contain a transposition? (There may be more than one possible answer.)

    a. Cash $170

    b. Cost of Goods Sold $2,300

    c. Taxes Payable $310

    d. Additional Paid-In Capital $1,200

5. Depreciation Expense for the building your company has owned for several years is listed on:

    a. the unadjusted trial balance
    b. the adjusted trial balance
    c. the post-closing trial balance
    d. all of the above

Problem II.

Fill in the blanks.

1. When an account balance seems to be in the wrong column on the trial balance, it may be an error—or it may be the correct balance of a(n) _____ _____.

2. The balance of an account is the side of the account—whether debit or credit—on which a(n) _____ is recorded.

3. A difference of $540 in the totals may be the result of a(n) _____ or _____.

4. If there is a Notes Payable balance on the adjusted trial balance, you would also expect to see two other accounts: _____ _____ and _____ _____.

Problem III.

1. Identify the source of the error on the adjusted trial balance, then correct the totals.

	Debit	Credit
Cash	$ 150	
Short-Term Investments	230	
Accounts Receivable	320	
Allowance for Doubtful Accounts		$ 20
Inventory	650	
Property, Plant and Equipment	2,700	
Accumulated Depreciation		850
Accounts Payable	100	
Bonds Payable		1,500
Discount on Bonds Payable	50	
Capital Stock		680
Retained Earnings		750
Revenues		1,000
Expenses	800	
Totals	$5,000	$4,800

2. Identify the source of the error on the adjusted trial balance, then correct the totals.

	Debit	Credit
Cash	$ 10	
Accounts Receivable	20	
Inventory	65	
Long-Term Investments	100	
Equipment	540	
Accumulated Depreciation		$200
Accounts Payable		20
Notes Payable		85
Capital Stock		200
Retained Earnings		40
Revenues		300
Expenses	200	
Totals	$935	$845

Problem IV.

List three errors that do *not* cause a difference in trial balance totals.

1. _____

2. _____

3. _____

Problem V.

The following adjusted trial balance totals were added by computer and are assumed to be correct. Find the errors in the trial balance, then create a new, correct adjusted trial balance.

	Debit	Credit
Cash	$ 1,200	
Accounts Receivable	1,700	
Allowance for Doubtful Accounts		$ 750
Inventory	4,200	
Prepaid Insurance		780
Investments	2,300	
Property, Plant and Equipment	13,400	
Accumulated Depreciation		2,800
Accounts Payable		1,300
Interest Payable		130
Bonds Payable		4,000
Capital Stock		10,000
Retained Earnings		3,500
Dividends	750	
Sales Revenue		21,000
Sales Discounts	340	
Interest Revenue		100
Purchases	13,000	
Purchase Discounts	160	
Selling Expense	470	
Salary Expense	3,600	
Depreciation Expense	860	
Administrative Expense	370	
Interest Expense	585	
Amortization Expense	10	
Gain on Sale of Equipment	500	
Totals	$43,445	$44,360

QUIZ 1   Solutions and Explanations

Problem I.

1. b

2. a

3. a

4. b *or* d
Total debits are $900 more than total credits. 9 first digit of the difference + 1 = 10. However, you cannot have a difference of 10 between two digits, so the number 1 is used. There are two account balances that may be the cause of the error: b. Cost of Goods Sold $2,300 (2 first digit – 3 second digit = 1), and d. Additional Paid-In Capital $1,200 (1 first digit – 2 second digit = 1).

5. b
Depreciation expense on the building your company owns is recorded in an adjusting entry and therefore does not appear on the unadjusted trial balance, but on the adjusted trial balance. In fact, it is called the *adjusted* trial balance because it includes the adjusting entries. Depreciation expense will not appear on the post-closing trial balance because it has been closed out with the other expense accounts.

Problem II.

1. contra account

2. increase

3. transposition; slide

4. Interest Payable; Interest Expense

Problem III.

1. The source of the $200 error is that Accounts Payable, a liability, has a credit balance of $100 that was listed in the debit column. This is a doubling error because it made total debits $100 too high *and* total credits $100 too low—for a total error of $200.

	Debit	Credit
Cash	$ 150	
Short-Term Investments	230	
Accounts Receivable	320	
Allowance for Doubtful Accounts		$ 20
Inventory	650	
Property, Plant and Equipment	2,700	
Accumulated Depreciation		850
Accounts Payable		**100**
Bonds Payable		1,500
Discount on Bonds Payable	50	
Capital Stock		680
Retained Earnings		750
Revenues		1,000
Expenses	800	
Totals	$4,900	$4,900

2. The $90 error may be a transposition or slide because it is divisible by 9 (90/9 = 10). However, the account balances seem reasonable, so the error is probably not a slide, but a it may be a transposition. It may be in Inventory or Equipment. It is not in Inventory because a transposition in this account would not make a difference of $90. However, if the account balance for Equipment is transposed, correcting it will decrease total debits by $90. A transposition in the Equipment account balance may be the source of the error.

	Debit	Credit
Cash	$ 10	
Accounts Receivable	20	
Inventory	65	
Long-Term Investments	100	
Equipment	**450**	
Accumulated Depreciation		$200
Accounts Payable		20
Notes Payable		85
Capital Stock		200
Retained Earnings		40
Revenues		300
Expenses	200	
Totals	$845	$845

Problem IV.

Three errors that do not cause a difference in trial balance totals are:

- a transaction not recorded on company books
- the same incorrect amount recorded on both the debit and credit side of a journal entry
- an amount recorded in an incorrect account that has the same debit or credit balance as the correct account (such as an amount debited to Rent Expense instead of Equipment or credited to Revenue instead of Accounts Payable).

Problem V.

There are several errors in this trial balance.

First, there are three account balances in the wrong columns:

1. The Prepaid Insurance balance of $780 should be listed as a debit because it is an asset (debit balance).

2. The Purchase Discounts balance of $160 should be listed as a credit because it is a contra account to Purchases, which is an expense (debit balance).

3. The Gain on Sale of Equipment balance of $500 should be listed as a credit because it is a revenue account (credit balance).

	Debit	Credit
Cash	$ 1,200	
Accounts Receivable	1,700	
Allowance for Doubtful Accounts		$ 750
Inventory	4,200	
Prepaid Insurance	**780**	
Investments	2,300	
Property, Plant and Equipment	13,400	
Accumulated Depreciation		2,800
Accounts Payable		1,300
Interest Payable		130
Bonds Payable		4,000
Capital Stock		10,000
Retained Earnings		3,500
Dividends	750	
Sales Revenue		21,000
Sales Discounts	340	
Interest Revenue		100
Purchases	13,000	
Purchase Discounts		**160**
Selling Expense	470	
Salary Expense	3,600	
Depreciation Expense	860	
Administrative Expense	370	
Interest Expense	585	
Amortization Expense	10	
Gain on Sale of Equipment		**500**
Totals	$43,565	$44,240

Second, even after the account balances are in the right columns, there is a $675 difference in the totals. Because this is divisible by 9 (675/9 = 75), check for a transposition or slide. If it is a transposition, the range is 7 (6 first digit + 1 = 7). But there are no account balances where the difference between the first two digits is 7. So check for a slide. Allowance for Doubtful Accounts has a balance of $750, almost half the Accounts Receivable balance, which is very unlikely. When corrected (750 – 75 = 675), the trial balance total debits equal total credits, as follows.

	Debit	Credit
Cash	$ 1,200	
Accounts Receivable	1,700	
Allowance for Doubtful Accounts		$ 75
Inventory	4,200	
Prepaid Insurance	**780**	
Investments	2,300	
Property, Plant and Equipment	13,400	
Accumulated Depreciation		2,800
Accounts Payable		1,300
Interest Payable		130
Bonds Payable		4,000
Capital Stock		10,000
Retained Earnings		3,500
Dividends	750	
Sales Revenue		21,000
Sales Discounts	340	
Interest Revenue		100
Purchases	13,000	
Purchase Discounts		**160**
Selling Expense	470	
Salary Expense	3,600	
Depreciation Expense	860	
Administrative Expense	370	
Interest Expense	585	
Amortization Expense	10	
Gain on Sale of Equipment		**500**
Totals	$43,565	$43,565

QUIZ 2   FINDING AND CORRECTING ERRORS USING THE UNADJUSTED TRIAL BALANCE

Problem I.

Multiple choice. Circle the correct answer.

1. Expense accounts . . .

    a. have a debit balance
    b. have a credit balance
    c. may have a debit balance or a credit balance
    d. appear only on the post-closing trial balance

2. Liability accounts . . .

    a. have a debit balance
    b. have a credit balance
    c. may have a debit balance or a credit balance
    d. appear only on the post-closing trial balance

3. Which of these errors can be detected on the unadjusted trial balance?

    a. failure to record an adjusting entry
    b. an overstated liability and an overstated expense
    c. a transaction that was not recorded
    d. none of these errors can be detected on the unadjusted trial balance

4. On the trial balance, total debits are $38,200 and total credits are $41,800. This error may have been caused by a transposition in . . .

    a. the Inventory balance of $920
    b. the Accumulated Depreciation balance of $7,300
    c. the Accounts Payable balance of $360
    d. the Retained Earnings balance of $2,600

5. Which of the following accounts may appear on all the unadjusted, adjusted and post-closing trial balances?

    a. Purchases
    b. Purchase Discounts
    c. Notes Payable
    d. all of the above

Problem II.

Fill in the blanks.

<u>Questions 1-3</u>: If the trial balance does not balance, the steps to take, in the correct order, are as follows:

1. Make sure the _____ _____ were correctly transferred to the _____ _____.

2. See if the _____ _____ _____ have been calculated correctly.

3. Check the _____ _____ and _____ for errors.

4. A contra account has a(n) _____ balance from its related account.

5. In the revenue section of the trial balance, you should not see a balance in the _____ column, unless it is for a revenue _____ _____.

6. If trial balance total debits are $70 more than total credits, there may be an error of $_____, caused by listing the $35 balance in the _____ column.

7. A post-closing trial balance should not include a(n) _____ account or a(n) _____ account.

Problem III.

Locate the error in the unadjusted trial balance and show correct totals.

	Debit	Credit
Cash	$ 40	
Accounts Receivable, net	60	
Inventory	90	
Property, Plant and Equipment	600	
Accumulated Depreciation		$ 200
Accounts Payable		400
Notes Payable		50
Capital Stock		300
Retained Earnings		100
Revenues		500
Expenses	400	
Totals	$1,190	$1,550

Problem IV.

The following adjusted trial balance totals were added by computer and are assumed to be correct. Find the errors in the trial balance, then create a new, correct adjusted trial balance.

	Debit	Credit
Cash	$ 7,770	
Accounts Receivable, net	13,000	
Interest Receivable	350	
Inventory	9,900	
Office Supplies	525	
Long-Term Notes Receivable	12,000	
Land	17,000	
Property, Plant and Equipment	98,000	
Accumulated Depreciation		$ 36,000
Patent, net		12,000
Accounts Payable		2,700
Interest Payable		940
Long-Term Notes Payable		24,000
Capital Stock		71,000
Retained Earnings		25,000
Dividends		1,200
Revenues		98,000
Interest Revenue		1,400
Purchases		19,000
Purchase Discounts		385
Wage and Salary Expense	34,000	
Rent Expense	9,100	
Depreciation Expense	12,000	
Administrative Expense	2,900	
Amortization Expense	800	
Interest Expense	2,800	
Loss on Sale of Equipment	780	
Totals	$220,925	$291,625

QUIZ 2 Solutions and Explanations

Problem I.

1. a

2. b

3. d

4. b
Either debits are understated by \$3,600 or credits are overstated by \$3,600. Eliminate Inventory and Accounts Payable because the error is too small.

Credit balances:

\$7,300	7,300 – 3,700 = 3,600 **D**
\$2,600	6,200 – 2,600 = 3,600 **I**

and

Total debits	**Total credits**
\$38,200	\$41,800
	– 3,600
\$38,200	\$38,200

5. c

Problem II.

1. account balances, trial balance

2. ledger account balances

3. journal entries, postings

4. opposite

5. debit; contra account

6. 35; debit

7. revenue; expense

Problem III.

The amount of the error is $360, which is divisible by 9. Examining the trial balance does not reveal the possibility of a transposition error. But there may be a slide error: Accounts Payable is much too large given the size of the other accounts, particularly with an Inventory balance of $90.

	Debit	Credit
Cash	$ 40	
Accounts Receivable, net	60	
Inventory	90	
Property, Plant and Equipment	600	
Accumulated Depreciation		$ 200
Accounts Payable		**40**
Notes Payable		50
Capital Stock		300
Retained Earnings		100
Revenues		500
Expenses	400	
Totals	$1,190	$1,190

Problem IV.

Three accounts are listed in the incorrect column for their balance. Patent, Dividends and Purchases should should all be listed in the debit column (see page 55, Figure 3-1).

After these are corrected, the trial balance remains out of balance by $6,300. This amount is divisible by 9 (6,300/9 = 700). If you look for a transposition error, the range will be 7, one more than 6, the first digit of the error amount. Looking at the account balances, you find only one account, Administrative Expense, whose first two digits differ by 7. When corrected (9,200 – 2,900 = 6,300), the trial balance total debits equal the total credits.

	Debit	Credit
Cash	$ 7,770	
Accounts Receivable, net	13,000	
Interest Receivable	350	
Inventory	9,900	
Office Supplies	525	
Long-Term Notes Receivable	12,000	
Land	17,000	
Property, Plant and Equipment	98,000	
Accumulated Depreciation		$ 36,000
Patent, net	**12,000**	
Accounts Payable		2,700
Interest Payable		940
Long-Term Notes Payable		24,000
Capital Stock		71,000
Retained Earnings		25,000
Dividends	**1,200**	
Revenues		98,000
Interest Revenue		1,400
Purchases	**19,000**	
Purchase Discounts		385
Wage and Salary Expense	34,000	
Rent Expense	9,100	
Depreciation Expense	12,000	
Administrative Expense	**9,200**	
Amortization Expense	800	
Interest Expense	2,800	
Loss on Sale of Equipment	780	
Totals	$259,425	$259,425

CORRECTING CURRENT PERIOD ACCRUAL ERRORS

Introduction

An accrual recognizes a revenue or expense before cash is received or paid. Although accrual errors may be discovered at any time, expenses that were not accrued are often found when they are paid, and revenues that were not accrued are often found when payment is received. Missing or inaccurate accruals may also be discovered when the financial statements are prepared. This section describes how to correct current period accrual errors. Keep in mind that the corrections explained here ignore tax effects.

Current Period Errors Defined

Current period errors are those made and found before the books for the period have been closed. These are the types of errors covered in this course.

How Current Period Errors Are Corrected

Current period accrual errors are easily corrected by adjusting the inaccurate account balances.

Prior Period Errors Defined

Prior period errors are those discovered after the books for that period have been closed. For example, if you discover an error that was made in last year's books and those books have been closed, it is a prior period error. Prior period errors affecting net income cannot be corrected simply by adjusting the incorrect revenue or expense accounts because these account balances no longer exist; they were reduced to zero (closed out) at the end of the period when net income was added to Retained Earnings. Correcting a prior period error requires a *prior period adjustment* to the Retained Earnings account (or Prior Period Adjustments account). Prior period adjustments are beyond the scope of this course.

Correcting Errors Involving Accrued Expenses and Accrued Revenues

As noted at the beginning of this section, how you correct an error depends on when you discover it. The following pages provide details on correcting current period accrual errors.

How to Correct Each Kind of Error

The examples shown in Figures 4-2 through 4-7 demonstrate how to correct each of the accrual errors listed below

---

Figure 4-1

Errors discovered before the books are closed

Expenses:

- Omission of an accrued expense

- Too little expense accrued

- Too much expense accrued

Revenues:

- Omission of an accrued revenue

- Too little revenue accrued

- Too much revenue accrued

ERRORS INVOLVING ACCRUED *EXPENSES*

Figure 4-2. Correcting <u>omission</u> of an accrued expense—discovered before the books are closed

On April 1, 20X0, your company took out an 8%, $25,000, 5-year note.

The error: Just before year end, you discover that the interest for the year of $1,500 ($25,000 x .08 x 9/12 of the year) has not been accrued.

To correct the error before the books are closed: Simply record the adjusting entry that was not made:

Interest Expense	1,500	
Interest Payable		1,500
(25,000 x .08 x 9/12 = 1,500)		

If this error were not corrected, it would have affected the 20X0 income statement and balance sheet as follows:

<u>Income statement</u>:

Interest expense	understated by	$1,500
Net income	overstated by	$1,500

<u>Balance sheet</u>:

Interest payable	understated by	$1,500
Retained earnings	overstated by	$1,500

ERRORS INVOLVING ACCRUED *EXPENSES*

Figure 4-3. Correcting accrual of <u>too little expense</u>—discovered before the books are closed.

On April 1, 20X0, your company took out a $25,000, 5-year note at 8% interest.

The error. Just before year-end 20X0, you discover that interest expense was mistakenly accrued for $1,200 instead of $1,500 ($25,000 x .08 x 9/12 of the year).

To correct the error before the books are closed: Record an adjusting entry for the missing amount:

<u>Original adjusting entry for too little expense:</u>

Interest Expense	1,200	
Interest Payable		1,200

<u>Additional adjusting entry to correct the error:</u>

Interest Expense	300	
Interest Payable		300

If this error were not corrected, it would have affected the 20X0 income statement and balance sheet as follows:

<u>Income statement:</u>

Interest expense	understated by	$300
Net income	overstated by	$300

<u>Balance sheet:</u>

Interest payable	understated by	$300
Retained earnings	overstated by	$300

ERRORS INVOLVING ACCRUED *EXPENSES*

Figure 4-4. Correcting accrual of <u>too much expense</u>—discovered before the books are closed.

On April 1, 20X0, your company took out a $25,000, 5-year note at 8% interest.

The error: Just before year-end 20X1, you discover that interest expense on the note was accrued for $2,000 instead of $1,500 (25,000 x .08 x 9/12 of the year).

To correct the error before the books are closed: Record an adjusting entry that reduces Interest Expense by the excess amount:

<u>Original adjusting entry for too much expense:</u>

Interest Expense	2,000	
Interest Payable		2,000

<u>Adjusting entry to correct the error:</u>

Interest Payable	500*	
Interest Expense		500**

*Reduces the payable by the $500 over-accrual.
**Reduces the expense by the $500 over-accrual.

If this error were not corrected, it would have affected the 20X0 income statement and balance sheet as follows:

<u>Income statement:</u>

Interest expense	overstated by	$500
Net income	understated by	$500

<u>Balance sheet:</u>

Interest payable	overstated by	$500
Retained earnings	understated by	$500

ERRORS INVOLVING ACCRUED *REVENUES*

Figure 4-5. Correcting <u>omission</u> of an accrued revenue—discovered before the books are closed.

On December 1, 20X0, your company sublet space to SmithCo for $900 per month. As of December 31, 20X0, SmithCo has not made any rental payments.

The error: Just before the 20X0 books are closed, you discover that the $900 rent for December was never accrued.

To correct the error before the books are closed: Record the adjusting entry that was not made:

Rent Receivable	900	
Rent Revenue		900

If this error were not corrected it would have affected the 20X0 income statement and balance sheet as follows:

<u>Income statement</u>:

Rent revenue	understated by	$900
Net income	understated by	$900

<u>Balance sheet</u>:

Rent receivable	understated by	$900
Retained earnings	understated by	$900

ERRORS INVOLVING ACCRUED *REVENUES*

Figure 4-6. Correcting accrual of <u>too little revenue</u>—discovered before the books are closed.

On December 1, 20X0, your company sublet space to SmithCo for $900 per month. As of December 31, 20X0, SmithCo has not made any rental payments.

The error: Just before the 20X0 books are closed, you discover that December's rent revenue was accrued for $500 instead of $900.

To correct the error before the books are closed: Record an adjusting entry for the missing amount:

<u>Original adjusting entry for too little revenue:</u>

Rent Receivable	500	
Rent Revenue		500

<u>Additional adjusting entry to correct the error:</u>

Rent Receivable	400	
Rent Revenue		400

If this error were not corrected, it would have affected the 20X0 financial statements as follows:

<u>Income statement:</u>

Rent revenue	understated by	$400
Net income	understated by	$400

<u>Balance sheet:</u>

Rent receivable	understated by	$400
Retained earnings	understated by	$400

ERRORS INVOLVING ACCRUED *REVENUES*

**Figure 4-7. Correcting accrual of <u>too much revenue</u>—discovered
before the books are closed.**

On December 1, 20X0, your company sublet space to SmithCo for $900 per month. As of
December 31, 20X0, SmithCo has not made any rental payments.

The error: Just before the books are closed for the year, you discover that rent revenue for
December was accrued for $1,200 instead of $900.

To correct the error before the books are closed: Record an adjusting entry that reduces
Rent Revenue by the excess amount:

<u>Original adjusting entry for too much revenue</u>:

Rent Receivable	1,200	
Rent Revenue		1,200

<u>Additional entry to correct the error</u>:

Rent Revenue	300	
Rent Receivable		300

If this error were not corrected, it would have affected the 20X0 financial statements as
follows:

<u>Income statement</u>:

Rent revenue	overstated by	$300
Net income	overstated by	$300

<u>Balance sheet</u>:

Rent receivable	overstated by	$300
Retained earnings	overstated by	$300

Reminder on Improperly Recorded Revenues and Expenses

What happens when a check is issued or received but not recorded, or is recorded for the wrong amount? These errors are found and corrected during the bank reconciliation. If, however, these types of errors are not found until the following year after the books are closed, follow the same procedures used for accruals that were omitted or recorded for the wrong amounts.

Summary

How an error is corrected depends on when it is discovered and which accounts are involved. Current period errors involving income statement accounts can be corrected by recording the entry or by adjusting the inaccurate accounts. Prior period errors involving income statement accounts are corrected with an adjustment to the Retained Earnings or Prior Period Adjustment accounts.

QUIZ 1   CORRECTING CURRENT PERIOD ACCRUAL ERRORS

Problem I.

Multiple choice. Circle the correct answer.

1. Current period errors are those made and found . . .

a. before the balance sheet accounts have been closed
b. before the income statement accounts have been closed
c. before either the balance sheet accounts or the income statement accounts have been closed
d. before December 31 of the year in which they occurred

2. A correcting entry is the same as the adjusting entry for errors when . . .

a. the books have been closed
b. the amount was recorded to an expense account
c. an expense was recorded to the wrong expense account
d. an expense that was not accrued is discovered before the books are closed

3. You discover before the books are closed that $800 of salary expense was not accrued. To correct this error, you would . . .

a. record $800 of salary expense when salaries are paid next period
b. simply record the accrual of $800 of salary expense before the books are closed
c. do nothing because accruals do not involve cash
d. wait until after the books are closed and then record the accrual of $800 of salary expense

4. Just before the books are closed you discover that $1,400 of interest expense was accrued when only $1,200 should have been accrued. To correct this error you would . . .

a. wait until the interest is paid next period and then record $200 of prepaid interest
b. do nothing because accruals do not involve cash
c. record an adjusting entry before the books are closed that reduces interest expense and interest payable by $200
d. next period do nothing this period but accrue $200 less interest expense after the books for this period are closed

Problem II.

Fill in the blanks.

1. If an accrued revenue is understated and the error is discovered in the same accounting period, a correction is made with a(n) _____ journal entry for the amount of the error.

2. An error not discovered until after the books have been closed is corrected with a(n) _____ _____ _____ .

3. If interest receivable was not accrued at the end of 20X1, then 20X1 revenues will be _____, and income will be _____.

4. If an accrual of rent expense was omitted at the end of 20X1, then 20X1 liabilities would be _____, and income would be _____.

Problem III.

1. In 20X4, accrued advertising expense of $7,500 was incorrectly recorded as $9,000.

   a. Show the correction for this error if it is discovered in 20X4.
   b. Show the effect of the error on the 20X4 income statement if the error is not discovered until 20X5.
   c. Show the effect of the error on the 20X4 balance sheet if it is not discovered until 20X5.

2. In 20X3, interest revenue of $1,000 was accrued; the correct amount was $800.

   a. Show the correction for this error if it is discovered in 20X3.
   b. Show the effect of the error on the 20X3 income statement if it is not discovered until 20X4.
   c. Show the effect of the error on the 20X3 balance sheet if it is not discovered until 20X4.

3. In 20X1, building supplies expense of $750 was accrued; it should have been $1,250.

    a. Show the correction for this error if it is discovered in 20X1.
    b. Show the effect of the error on the 20X1 income statement if it is not discovered until 20X2.
    c. Show the effect of the error on the 20X1 balance sheet if it is not discovered until 20X2.

4. In 20X0, interest revenue of $110 was accrued when it should have been $200.

    a. Show the correction for this error if it is discovered in 20X0.
    b. Show the effect of the error on the 20X0 income statement if it is not discovered until 20X1.
    c. Show the effect of the error on the 20X0 balance sheet if it is not discovered until 20X1.

QUIZ 1   Solutions and Explanations

Problem I.

      1. b

      2. d

      3. b

      4. c

Problem II.

      1. adjusting

      2. prior period adjustment

      3. understated; understated

      4. understated; overstated

Problem III.

1. In 20X4, accrued advertising expense of $7,500 was incorrectly recorded as $9,000.

a. The correction for this error if it is discovered in the same year (20X4) is a simple entry to reduce the amount of the overstatement:

Advertising Payable	1,500	
Advertising Expense		1,500

b. The effect of the error on the 20X4 income statement if it is not discovered until 20X5 is as follows:

Advertising expense	overstated by	$1,500
Net income	understated by	$1,500

c. The effect of the error on the 20X4 balance sheet if it is not discovered until 20X5 is as follows:

Advertising Payable	overstated by	1,500
Retained earnings	understated by	1,500

2. In 20X3, interest revenue of $1,000 was accrued; the correct amount was $800.

a. The correction for this error when discovered in the same year (20X3) is a simple entry that reverses the overstatement:

Interest Revenue	200	
Interest Receivable		200

b. The effect of the error on the 20X3 income statement if it is not discovered until 20X4 is as follows:

Interest revenue	overstated by	$200
Net income	overstated by	$200

c. The effect of the error on the 20X3 balance sheet if it is not discovered until 20X4 is as follows:

Interest receivable	overstated by	$200
Retained earnings	overstated by	200

3. In 20X1, building supplies expense of $750 was accrued when it should have been $1,250.

a. The correction for this error if it is discovered in the same year (20X1) is simply an adjusting entry for the missing amount:

Building Supplies Expense	500	
Building Supplies Payable		500

b. The effect of the error on the 20X1 income statement if it is not discovered until 20X2 is as follows:

Building supplies expense	understated by	$500
Net income	overstated by	$500

c. The effect of the error on the 20X1 balance sheet if it is not discovered until 20X2 is as follows:

Building supplies payable	understated by	$500
Retained earnings	overstated by	$500

4. In 20X0, interest revenue of $110 was accrued when it should have been $200.

a. The correction for this error if it is discovered in the same year (20X0) is a simple adjusting entry for the additional amount required:

Interest Receivable	90	
Interest Revenue		90

b. The effect of the error on the 20X0 income statement if it is not discovered until 20X1 is as follows:

Interest revenue	understated by	$90
Net income	understated by	$90

c. The effect of the error on the 20X0 balance sheet if it is not discovered until 20X1 is as follows:

Interest Receivable	understated by	$90
Retained earnings	understated by	$90

QUIZ 2   CORRECTING CURRENT PERIOD ACCRUAL ERRORS

Problem I.

Multiple choice. Circle the correct answer.

1. Missing or inaccurate accruals are often found . . .

   a. when an expense is paid
   b. when revenue is received
   c. when the financial statements are prepared
   d. all of the above

2. A more precise definition of prior period error would include one that is found . . .

   a. after the income statement accounts have been closed for the year in which the errors were made
   b. after the balance sheet accounts have been closed for the year in which the errors were made
   c. after either the balance sheet accounts or the income statement accounts have been closed for the year in which the errors were made
   d. after December 31 of the year in which they occurred

3. In 20X1, the accrual of rent expense was overstated by $1,000. A correcting entry made before the books are closed would include:

   a. a debit to Rent Expense for $1,000
   b. a credit to Rent Expense for $1,000
   c. a credit to Rent Payable for $1,000
   d. a credit to Cash for $1,000

Problem II.

Fill in the blanks.

1. _____ period errors affect revenue and expense accounts that are still open.

2. Accounting error correction depends on the _____ in which the error is discovered.

3. Errors that affect revenue or expense accounts from prior periods cannot be directly corrected because these account balances have been _____.

4. If wages payable were not accrued at the end of 20X1, then 20X1 expenses were _____ and 20X1 net income was _____.

5. Failure to accrue interest revenue during the current year will result in an understatement of the two balance sheet accounts _____ and _____.

Problem III.

1. Advertising expense of $4,000 was not accrued at the end of 20X1. The error was discovered on January 6, 20X2 before the books for 20X1 were closed.

   a. What kind of error is this?
   b. What is the correcting entry to be recorded on January 6, 20X2?

2. The error made in question 1 was not discovered until May 2, 20X2 after the 20X1 books were closed.

   a. What kind of error is this?
   b. What is its impact on the 20X1 income statement?
   c. What is its impact on the 20X1 balance sheet?

QUIZ 2 Solutions and Explanations

Problem I.

1. d

2. a

3. b

Problem II.

1. current

2. period

3. closed

4. understated; overstated

5. Interest Receivable; Retained Earnings. As a result of Interest Receivable being understated, net income will also be understated, and when net income is closed out to Retained Earnings, Retained Earnings will be understated as well.

Problem III.

1. a. This is a current period error because the books for the period in which the error was made have not been closed.

b. The correcting entry is an adjusting entry for the amount of the error:

Advertising Expense	4,000	
Advertising Payable		4,000

2. a. This is a prior period error because the books for the period in which the error was made have not been closed.

b. The effect of the error on the 20X1 income statement if it is not discovered until 20X2 is as follows:

Advertising expense	understated by	$4,000
Net income	overstated by	$4,000

c. The effect of the error on the 20X1 balance sheet if it is not discovered until 20X2 is as follows:

Advertising payable	understated by	$4,000
Retained earnings	overstated by	$4,000

Section 5

CORRECTING CURRENT PERIOD DEFERRAL ERRORS

Introduction

A deferral is cash received or paid before it is recognized as a revenue or an expense. Deferral errors affect both the income statement and the balance sheet. This section describes how to correct current period deferral errors. Keep in mind that the corrections explained here ignore tax effects.

The Basics of Deferred Expenses

Deferred, or prepaid, expenses are those that a company pays in advance for services or goods it will use over more than one accounting period. The portion used in the current period is the expense; the remaining portion is put off, or *deferred*, for use in a future period. For example, say that on November 1, your company makes a three-month prepayment for a magazine ad. The portion paid for November and December is an expense because it is used in the current year; the portion paid for January is a deferred expense because it will be used in the next year.

- **Recording prepayment of expenses.** When your company makes a prepayment, you credit Cash, but you can debit either of two accounts:

  - 1. You can debit an expense account, such as Rent Expense, Office Supplies Expense or Advertising Expense; or

  - 2. You can debit a prepaid asset account, such as Prepaid Rent, Prepaid Office Supplies or Prepaid Advertising Expense.

- **Recording the year-end adjustment for deferred expenses.** The year-end adjustment will depend on which account you chose to record the prepayment. To figure out the right adjusting journal entry (AJE), you need to ask the right question:

  - 1. If you recorded the prepayment to an expense account, ask: *"By what amount must the expense account balance be reduced to show only the expense used up in the current period?"*

- 2. If you recorded the prepayment to a prepaid asset account, ask: *"How much of the prepaid asset account balance must be transferred to the expense account to show the amount used up in the current period?"*

The Basics of Deferred Revenues

Deferred, or unearned, revenues are those that a company receives for services that it will perform or for goods that it will deliver over more than one accounting period. The portion earned in the current period for the services or goods delivered in the current period is revenue; the remaining portion is put off, or deferred, to be earned in a future period. For example, on December 1 your company receives a three-month rental prepayment for space it is subletting. The portion for December is revenue because it is earned in the current year; the portion for January and February is deferred revenue—usually referred to as *unearned revenue* or *revenue received in advance* because it will not be earned until the next year.

- **Recording revenue received in advance.** When your company receives an advance payment, you debit Cash, but you can credit either of two accounts:

  - 1. You can credit a revenue account, such as Rent Revenue or Subscription Revenue, or

  - 2. You can credit a liability account, such as Unearned Rent Revenue, Unearned Fees, or Rent Received in Advance.

- **Recording the year-end adjustment for deferred revenue.** The year-end adjustment will depend on which account you chose to record the advance payment. To figure out the AJE, you need to ask the right question.

  - 1. If you recorded the revenue in advance to a revenue account, ask: *"By what amount must the revenue account balance be reduced to show only the revenue earned in the current period?"*

  - 2. If you recorded the advance payment in a liability account (Unearned [Various account titles]) ask: *"How much of the liability account balance must be transferred to the revenue account to show the amount earned in the current period?"*

Current v. Prior Period Errors

Current period errors are errors made and found before the books for the period have been closed. The corrections are made by recording the necessary adjusting entry. These are the types of errors covered in this course.

Prior period errors are those discovered after the books for the period in which the error was made are closed. For example, if an error is made in 20X4 but is not discovered until 20X5 after the 20X4 books are closed, it is a prior period error. If the error involves 20X4 revenue or expense accounts, it cannot be corrected by adjusting 20X4 revenue or expense account balances because they were closed to produce 20X4 net income. Correcting this error requires a prior period adjustment.

Correcting Deferral Errors

Examples are provided for each of the errors shown in Figure 5-1.

Correcting Each Kind of Error

Figures 5-2 through 5-13 show examples of how to correct each of the errors listed on the next page.

Figure 5-1

Errors discovered before the books are closed

Prepayment originally recorded as an expense

- Failure to recognize the correct amount of expense and to defer the unused portion

- Too little expense recognized, too much deferred

- Too much expense recognized, too little deferred

Prepayment originally recorded as a prepaid asset

- Failure to recognize the correct amount of expense and to defer the unused portion

- Too little expense recognized, too much deferred

- Too much expense recognized, too little deferred

Payment received in advance originally recorded as revenue

- Failure to recognize the correct amount of revenue earned and to defer the portion not yet earned

- Too little revenue recognized, too much deferred

- Too much revenue recognized, too little deferred

Prepayment received in advance originally recorded as revenue received in advance (or unearned revenue)

- Failure to recognize the correct amount of revenue earned and to defer the portion not yet earned

- Too little revenue recognized, too much deferred

- Too much revenue recognized, too little deferred

ERRORS INVOLVING A PREPAYMENT
ORIGINALLY RECORDED AS AN *EXPENSE*

Figure 5-2. Correcting the failure to recognize the correct amount of expense and to defer the unused portion—discovered before the books are closed.

On March 1, 20X0, your company took out a 2-year insurance policy at $3,000 per year. The firm prepaid the entire amount, recording it as an <u>expense</u>.

Transaction entry on 3/1/20X0

Insurance Expense	6,000	
Cash		6,000

The error: You discover that there is no end-of-year AJE reducing Insurance Expense to the amount used in 20X0 and deferring the unused portion.

To correct the error before the books are closed: The question is—by what amount must Insurance Expense be reduced to show only the expense used up (recognized) in 20X0?

1. <u>To compute 20X0 insurance expense:</u> $6,000 prepayment/24 months = $250 per month x 10 months (March-December, 20X0) = $2,500 insurance expense used up in 20X0.

2. <u>To compute the reduction needed in Insurance Expense:</u> $6,000 prepayment – $2,500 expense used up in 20X1 = $3,500 reduction needed in Insurance Expense; the same amount is deferred to Prepaid Insurance.

Correcting entry to record before the books are closed

Prepaid Insurance	**3,500**	
Insurance Expense		**3,500**

The balance in Insurance Expense is computed as follows: $6,000 balance from March prepayment – $3,500 credit in the correcting (adjusting) entry = $2,500 balance—the amount of insurance expense used up in 20X0.

This correcting entry is the adjusting entry that should have been made.

If the error were not corrected before the books were closed, it would affect the 20X0 income statement and balance sheet as follows:

Income statement:

Insurance expense	overstated by	$3,500
Net income	understated by	$3,500

Balance sheet:

Prepaid insurance	understated by	$3,500
Retained earnings	understated by	$3,500

ERRORS INVOLVING A PREPAYMENT
ORIGINALLY RECORDED AS AN *EXPENSE*

Figure 5-3. Correcting too little expense recognized, too much deferred—discovered before the books are closed.

On March 1, 20X0, your company took out a 2-year insurance policy at $3,000 per year. It prepaid the entire amount, recording it as an <u>expense</u>.

Transaction entry on 3/1/20X0

Insurance Expense	6,000	
Cash		6,000

The error: You discover that the end-of-year AJE resulted in too little expense being recognized and too much being deferred:

AJE on 12/31/20X0

Prepaid Insurance	5,000	
Insurance Expense		5,000

To correct the error before the books are closed: The question is—by what amount should Insurance Expense have been reduced to show only the expense used up (recognized) in 20X0?

1. <u>To compute 20X0 insurance expense</u>: $6,000 prepayment/24 months = $250 per month x 10 months (March-December, 20X0) = $2,500 insurance expense used up in 20X0.

2. <u>To compute the reduction that should have been made in Insurance Expense</u>: $6,000 prepayment – $2,500 expense used in 20X0 = $3,500 reduction that should have been made in Insurance Expense and deferred to Prepaid Insurance for future use.

3. <u>To compute the correction</u>: $5,000 incorrect AJE reduction in Insurance Expense – $3,500 correct amount = $1,500 correction (the amount that must be added back to Insurance Expense).

Correcting entry to record before the books are closed

Insurance Expense	**1,500**	
Prepaid Insurance		**1,500**

This entry leaves the correct Insurance Expense balance of $2,500 ($1,000 balance from AJE + $1,500 added back = $2,500 correct balance) and defers the correct amount of $3,500 to Prepaid Insurance ($5,000 balance from AJE – $1,500 reduction = $3,500 correct balance).

If the error were not corrected before the books were closed, it would affect the 20X0 income statement and balance sheet as follows:

Income statement:

Insurance expense	understated by	$1,500
Net income	overstated by	$1,500

Balance sheet:

Prepaid Insurance	overstated by	$1,500
Retained earnings	overstated by	$1,500

ERRORS INVOLVING A PREPAYMENT
ORIGINALLY RECORDED AS AN *EXPENSE*

Figure 5-4. Correcting too much expense recognized, too little deferred—discovered before the books are closed.

On March 1, 20X0, your company took out a 2-year insurance policy at $3,000 per year. The firm prepaid the entire amount, recording it as an **expense.**

Transaction entry on 3/1/20X0

Insurance Expense	6,000	
Cash		6,000

The error: You discover that the end-of-year AJE resulted in too much expense being recognized and too little being deferred:

AJE on 12/31/20X0

Prepaid Insurance	500	
Insurance Expense		500

To correct the error before the books are closed: The question is—by what amount should Insurance Expense have been reduced to show only the expense used up (recognized) in 20X0?

1. To compute 20X0 insurance expense: $6,000 prepayment/24 months = $250 per month x 10 months (March–December, 20X0) = $2,500 insurance expense used up in 20X0.

2. To compute the reduction that should have been made in Insurance Expense: $6,000 prepayment – $2,500 expense used up in 20X0 = $3,500 reduction that should have been made in Insurance Expense and deferred to Prepaid Insurance for future use.

3. To compute the correction: $3,500 correct AJE reduction in Insurance Expense – $500 reduction already made in AJE = $3,000 more that must be deducted.

Correcting entry to record before the books are closed

Prepaid Insurance	**3,000**	
Insurance Expense		**3,000**

This entry leaves the correct Insurance Expense balance of $2,500 ($5,500 balance from AJE – $3,000 reduction from correcting entry = $2,500 correct balance) and defers the correct amount of $3,500 to Prepaid Insurance ($500 balance from AJE + $3,000 addition from correcting entry = $3,500 correct balance).

If the error were not corrected before the books were closed, it would affect the 20X0 income statement and balance sheet as follows:

Income statement:

Insurance expense	overstated by	$3,000
Net income	understated by	$3,000

Balance sheet:

Prepaid insurance	understated by	$3,000
Retained earnings	understated by	$3,000

ERRORS INVOLVING A PREPAYMENT
ORIGINALLY RECORDED AS A *PREPAID ASSET*

Figure 5-5. Correcting the failure to recognize the correct amount of expense and to defer the unused portion—discovered before the books are closed.

In March 1, 20X0, your company took out a 2-year insurance policy at $3,000 per year. The firm prepaid the entire amount, recording it as a prepayment.

Transaction entry on 3/1/20X0

Prepaid Insurance	6,000	
Cash		6,000

The error: You discover that there is no end-of-year AJE to recognize 20X0 insurance expense and to reduce Prepaid Insurance to the amount that should be deferred for future use.

To correct the error before the books are closed: The question is—how much of the Prepaid Insurance balance must be transferred to Insurance Expense to show the amount used up (recognized) in the current period?

1. To compute 20X0 insurance expense: $6,000 prepayment/24 months = $250 per month x 10 months (March–December, 20X0) = $2,500 insurance expense used up in 20X0.

2. To compute the 20X0 balance in Prepaid Insurance: $6,000 prepayment – $2,500 insurance expense = $3,500 remaining in Prepaid Insurance (the amount deferred for future use).

Correcting entry to record before the books are closed

Insurance Expense	**2,500**	
Prepaid Insurance		**2,500**

This correcting entry is the adjusting entry that had not been made.

If the error were not corrected before the books were closed, it would affect the 20X0 income statement and balance sheet as follows:

Income statement:

Insurance expense	understated by	$2,500
Net income	overstated by	$2,500

Balance sheet:

Prepaid insurance	overstated by	$2,500
Retained earnings	overstated by	$2,500

ERRORS INVOLVING A PREPAYMENT
ORIGINALLY RECORDED AS A *PREPAID ASSET*

Figure 5-6. Correcting too little expense recognized, too much deferred—discovered before the books are closed.

On March 1, 20X0, your company took out a 2-year insurance policy at $3,000 per year. It prepaid the entire amount, recording it as a <u>prepayment</u>.

Transaction entry on 3/1/20X0

Prepaid Insurance	6,000	
Cash		6,000

The error: You discover that the end-of-year AJE resulted in too little expense being recognized and too much being deferred:

AJE on 12/31/20X0

Insurance Expense	500	
Prepaid Insurance		500

To correct the error before the books are closed: The question is—how much of the Prepaid Insurance balance should have been transferred to Insurance Expense to show the amount used up (recognized) in the current period?

1. <u>To compute 20X0 insurance expense</u>: $6,000 prepayment/24 months = $250 per month x 10 months (March–December, 20X0) = $2,500 insurance expense used up in 20X0.

2. To compute <u>the correction</u>: $2,500 correct increase in to Insurance Expense – $500 AJE increase = $2,000 more must be added.

Correcting entry to record before the books are closed

Insurance Expense	**2,000**	
Prepaid Insurance		**2,000**

This entry leaves the correct Insurance Expense balance of $2,500 ($500 balance from AJE + $2,000 added to it in correcting entry = $2,500 correct balance) and leaves the correct amount of $3,500 in Prepaid Insurance to be deferred for future use ($5,500 balance from AJE – $2,000 reduction = $3,500 correct balance).

If the error were not corrected before the books were closed, it would affect the 20X0 income statement and balance sheet as follows:

<u>Income statement</u>:

Insurance expense	understated by	$2,000
Net income	overstated by	$2,000

<u>Balance sheet</u>:

Prepaid insurance	overstated by	$2,000
Retained earnings	overstated by	$2,000

ERRORS INVOLVING A PREPAYMENT
ORIGINALLY RECORDED AS A *PREPAID ASSET*

Figure 5-7. Correcting too much expense recognized, too little deferred—discovered before the books are closed.

On March 1, 20X0, your company took out a 2-year insurance policy at $3,000 per year. The firm prepaid the entire amount, recording it as a <u>prepayment</u>.

<u>Transaction entry on 3/1/20X0</u>

Prepaid Insurance	6,000	
Cash		6,000

The error: You discover that the end-of-year AJE resulted in too much expense being recognized and too little being deferred:

<u>AJE on 12/31/20X0</u>

Insurance Expense	4,000	
Prepaid Insurance		4,000

To correct the error before the books are closed: The question is—how much of the Prepaid Insurance balance should have been transferred to Insurance Expense to show the amount used up (recognized) in the current period?

1. <u>To compute 20X0 insurance expense</u>: $6,000 prepayment/24 months = $250 per month x 10 months (March–December, 20X0) = $2,500 insurance expense used up in 20X0.

2. <u>To compute the correction</u>: $4,000 transferred to Insurance Expense in the AJE – $2,500 insurance expense used up in 20X0 = $1,500 reduction needed in Insurance Expense (the same amount is also transferred back to Prepaid Insurance to be used in the future).

<u>Correcting entry to record before the books are closed</u>

Prepaid Insurance	1,500	
Insurance Expense		1,500

This entry corrects the Insurance Expense balance to $2,500 ($4,000 balance from AJE – $1,500 reduction from correcting entry = $2,500 correct balance) and leaves the correct amount of $3,500 in Prepaid Insurance to be deferred for future use ($2,000 balance after AJE + $1,500 increase = $3,500 correct balance).

If the error were not corrected before the books were closed, it would affect the 20X0 income statement and balance sheet as follows:

<u>Income statement</u>:

Insurance expense	overstated by	$1,500
Net income	understated by	$1,500

<u>Balance sheet</u>:

Prepaid insurance	understated by	$1,500
Retained earnings	understated by	$1,500

ERRORS INVOLVING A PAYMENT RECEIVED
IN ADVANCE ORIGINALLY RECORDED AS *REVENUE*.

**Figure 5-8. Correcting the failure to recognize the correct amount
of revenue earned and to defer the portion not yet
earned—discovered before the books are closed.**

On November 1, 20X0, your company sublet space for $800 per month. You received a
check for $4,000 for 5 months' rent in advance—November, December, January, February,
and March—that you recorded as <u>revenue</u>.

Transaction entry on 11/1/20X0

Cash	4,000	
Rent Revenue		4,000

The error: You discover that there is no end-of-year AJE to reduce Rent Revenue to the
amount earned in 20X0 and to defer the unused portion.

To correct the error before the books are closed: The question is—by what amount must
Rent Revenue be reduced to show only the amount earned in the current period?

1. To compute 20X0 rent revenue earned: $4,000 prepayment/5 months = $800 per month
   x 2 months (November–December, 20X0) = $1,600 rent revenue earned in 20X0.

2. To compute the reduction needed in Rent Revenue: $4,000 prepayment – $1,600 rent
   revenue earned in 20X0 = $2,400 reduction needed in Rent Revenue; the same amount
   is deferred to Rent Received in Advance (or Unearned Rent Revenue) for future use.

Correcting entry to record before the books are closed

Rent Revenue	**2,400**	
Rent Received in Advance		**2,400**

The balance in Rent Revenue is computed as follows: $4,000 balance from November re-
ceipt of revenue received in advance – $2,400 debit = $1,600 balance—the amount of rent
revenue earned in 20X0.

This correcting entry is the adjusting entry that had not been made.

If the error were not corrected before the books were closed, it would affect the 20X0 income statement and balance sheet as follows:

Income statement:

Rent revenue	overstated by	$2,400
Net income	overstated by	$2,400

Balance sheet:

Rent received in advance	understated by	$2,400
Retained earnings	overstated by	$2,400

ERRORS INVOLVING A PAYMENT RECEIVED IN ADVANCE
ORIGINALLY RECORDED AS *REVENUE*

**Figure 5-9. Correcting too little revenue recognized, too much
deferred—discovered before the books are closed.**

On November 1, 20X0, your company sublet space for $800 per month. You received a
check for $4,000 for 5 months' rent in advance—November, December, January, February,
and March—that you recorded as <u>revenue</u>.

> Transaction entry on 11/1/20X0
>
> | | | |
> |---|---|---|
> | Cash | 4,000 | |
> | Rent Revenue | | 4,000 |

The error: You discover that the end-of-year AJE resulted in too little revenue being recognized and too much being deferred.

> AJE on 12/31/20X0
>
> | | | |
> |---|---|---|
> | Rent Revenue | 3,200 | |
> | Rent Received in Advance | | 3,200 |

To correct the error before the books are closed: The question is—by what amount should
Rent Revenue have been reduced to show only the amount earned in the current period?

1. <u>To compute 20X0 rent revenue earned</u>: $4,000 prepayment/5 months = $800 per month
   x 2 months (November–December, 20X0) = $1,600 rent revenue earned in 20X0.

2. <u>To compute the reduction needed in Rent Revenue</u>: $4,000 prepayment – $1,600
   revenue earned in 20X0 = $2,400 reduction should have been made in Rent Revenue and
   deferred to Rent Received in Advance (or Unearned Rent Revenue) for future periods.

3. <u>To compute the correction</u>: $3,200 incorrect AJE reduction in Rent Revenue – $2,400
   correct amount = $800 correction—the amount that must be added back to Rent Revenue.

> <u>Correcting entry to record before the books are closed</u>
>
> | | | |
> |---|---|---|
> | **Rent Received in Advance** | **800** | |
> | **Rent Revenue** | | **800** |

This entry leaves the correct balance in Rent Revenue of $1,600 ($800 balance remaining
after AJE + $800 added back = $1,600 correct remaining balance) and defers the correct
amount of $2,400 to Rent Received in Advance ($3,200 balance from incorrect AJE – $800
reduction = $2,400 correct balance) to be earned in future periods.

If the error were not corrected before the books were closed, it would affect the 20X0 income statement and balance sheet as follows:

> <u>Income statement:</u>
>
> | | | |
> |---|---|---|
> | Rent revenue | understated by | $800 |
> | Net income | understated by | $800 |
>
> <u>Balance sheet:</u>
>
> | | | |
> |---|---|---|
> | Rent received in advance | overstated by | $800 |
> | Retained earnings | understated by | $800 |

ERRORS INVOLVING A PAYMENT RECEIVED IN ADVANCE ORIGINALLY RECORDED AS *REVENUE*

Figure 5-10. Correcting too much revenue recognized, too little deferred—discovered before the books are closed.

On November 1, 20X0, your company sublet space for $800 per month. You received a check for $4,000 for 5 months' rent in advance—November, December, January, February, and March—that you recorded as <u>revenue</u>.

Transaction entry on 11/1/20X0

Cash	4,000	
Rent Revenue		4,000

The error: You discover that the end-of-year AJE resulted in too much revenue being recognized and too little being deferred:

AJE on 12/31/20X0

Rent Revenue	800	
Rent Received in Advance		800

To correct the error before the books are closed: The question is—by what amount should Rent Revenue have been reduced to show only the amount earned in the current period?

1. <u>To compute 20X0 rent revenue earned:</u> $4,000 prepayment/5 months = $800 per month x 2 months (November–December, 20X0) = $1,600 rent revenue earned in 20X0.

2. <u>To compute the reduction needed in Rent Revenue:</u> $4,000 prepayment – $1,600 revenue earned in 20X0 – $2,400 reduction should have been made in Rent Revenue and deferred to Rent Received in Advance (or Unearned Rent Revenue) for future periods.

3. <u>To compute the correction:</u> $2,400 correct reduction in Rent Revenue – $800 incorrect AJE reduction = $1,600 that must be deducted from Rent Revenue.

Correcting entry to record before the books are closed

Rent Revenue	**1,600**	
Rent Received in Advance		**1,600**

This entry leaves the correct Rent Revenue balance of $1,600 ($3,200 balance from AJE – $1,600 reduction = $1,600 correct balance) and defers the correct amount of $2,400 to Rent Received in Advance ($800 balance from AJE + $1,600 added back = $2,400 correct balance) to be earned in future periods.

If the error were not corrected before the books were closed, it would affect the 20X0 income statement and balance sheet as follows:

Income statement:

Rent revenue	overstated by	$1,600
Net income	overstated by	$1,600

Balance sheet:

Rent received in advance	understated by	$1,600
Retained earnings	overstated by	$1,600

ERRORS INVOLVING A PREPAYMENT ORIGINALLY RECORDED AS *REVENUE RECEIVED IN ADVANCE* (OR UNEARNED REVENUE)

Figure 5-11. Correcting the failure to recognize the correct amount of expense and to defer the unused portion—discovered before the books are closed.

On November 1, 20X0, your company sublet space for $800 per month. You received a check for $4,000 for 5 months' rent in advance—November, December, January, February, and March—that you recorded as <u>revenue received in advance</u>.

Transaction entry on 11/1/20X0

Cash	4,000	
Rent Received in Advance		4,000

The error: You discover that there is no end-of-year AJE to recognize 20X0 rent revenue and to reduce the balance in Rent Received in Advance to the amount that will be earned in future periods (deferred).

To correct the error before the books are closed: The question is—how much of the liability account balance (Rent Received in Advance) must be transferred to the revenue account to show the amount earned in the current period?

1. <u>To compute 20X0 rent revenue earned</u>: $4,000 prepayment/5 months = $800 per month x 2 months (November–December, 20X0) = $1,600 rent revenue earned in 20X0.

2. <u>To compute the 20X0 balance in Rent Received in Advance</u>: $4,000 prepayment – $1,600 rent revenue = $2,400 remaining in Rent Received in Advance for future periods.

Correcting entry to record before the books are closed

Rent Received in Advance	**1,600**	
Rent Revenue		**1,600**

This correcting entry is the adjusting entry that had not been made.

If the error were not corrected before the books were closed, it would affect the 20X0 income statement and balance sheet as follows:

<u>Income statement</u>:

Rent revenue	understated by	$1,600
Net income	understated by	$1,600

<u>Balance sheet</u>:

Rent received in advance	overstated by	$1,600
Retained earnings	understated by	$1,600

ERRORS INVOLVING A PREPAYMENT ORIGINALLY RECORDED AS *REVENUE RECEIVED IN ADVANCE* (OR UNEARNED REVENUE)

Figure 5-12. Correcting too little revenue recognized, too much deferred—discovered before the books are closed.

On November 1, 20X0, your company sublet space for $800 per month. You received a check for $4,000 for 5 months' rent in advance—November, December, January, February, and March—that you recorded as <u>revenue received in advance</u>.

Transaction entry on 11/1/20X0
Cash	4,000	
Rent Received in Advance		4,000

The error: You discover that the end-of-year AJE resulted in too little revenue being recognized and too much being deferred:

AJE on 12/31/20X0
Rent Received in Advance	800	
Rent Revenue		800

To correct the error before the books are closed: The question is—how much of the Rent Received in Advance balance should have been transferred to Rent Revenue to show the amount earned in the current period?

1. <u>To compute 20X0 rent revenue earned</u>: $4,000 prepayment/5 months = $800 per month x 2 months (November–December, 20X0) = $1,600 rent revenue earned in 20X0.

2. <u>To compute the 20X0 balance in Rent Received in Advance</u>: $4,000 prepayment – $1,600 rent revenue = $2,400 remaining in Rent Received in Advance for future periods.

3. <u>To compute the correction</u>: $1,600 correct reduction in Rent Received in Advance – $800 incorrect AJE reduction = $800 more that must be transferred to Rent Revenue.

Correcting entry to record before the books are closed
Rent Received in Advance	**800**	
Rent Revenue		**800**

This entry leaves the correct balance of $1,600 in Rent Revenue ($800 balance from AJE + $800 from correcting entry = $1,600 correct balance) and the correct balance of $2,400 in Rent Received in Advance ($3,200 incorrect balance from AJE – $800 reduction = $2,400 correct balance) to be earned in future periods.

If the error were not corrected before the books were closed, it would affect the 20X0 income statement and balance sheet is as follows:

Income statement:
Rent revenue	understated by	$800
Net income	understated by	$800

Balance sheet:
Rent received in advance	overstated by	$800
Retained earnings	understated by	$800

ERRORS INVOLVING A PREPAYMENT ORIGINALLY RECORDED AS *REVENUE RECEIVED IN ADVANCE* (OR UNEARNED REVENUE)

Figure 5-13. Correcting too much revenue recognized, too little deferred—discovered before the books are closed.

On November 1, 20X0, your company sublet space for $800 per month. You received a check for $4,000 for 5 months' rent in advance—November, December, January, February, and March—that you recorded as <u>revenue received in advance</u>.

<u>Transaction entry on 11/1/20X0</u>

Cash	4,000	
Rent Received in Advance		4,000

The error: You discover that the end-of-year AJE resulted in too much revenue being recognized and too little being deferred:

<u>AJE on 12/31/20X0</u>

Rent Received in Advance	2,400	
Rent Revenue		2,400

To correct the error before the books are closed: The question is—how much of the Rent Received in Advance balance should have been transferred to Rent Revenue to show the amount earned in 20X0?

1. <u>To compute 20X0 rent revenue earned</u>: $4,000 prepayment/5 months = $800 per month x 2 months (November–December, 20X0) = $1,600 rent revenue earned in 20X0.

2. <u>To compute the 20X0 balance in Rent Received in Advance</u>: $4,000 prepayment – $1,600 rent revenue = $2,400 remaining in Rent Received in Advance for future periods.

3. <u>To compute the correction</u>: $2,400 incorrect AJE reduction – $1,600 correct reduction = $800 to be added back to Rent Received in Advance.

<u>Correcting entry to record before the books are closed</u>

Rent Revenue	**800**	
Rent Received in Advance		**800**

This entry leaves the correct Rent Revenue balance of $1,600 ($2,400 balance from AJE – $800 deduction = $1,600 correct balance) and defers the correct amount of $2,400 to Rent Received in Advance ($1,600 balance from AJE + $800 added back = $2,400 correct balance) to be earned in future periods.

If the error were not corrected before the books were closed, it would affect the 20X0 income statement and balance sheet as follows:

<u>Income statement</u>:

Rent revenue	overstated by	$800
Net income	overstated by	$800

<u>Balance sheet</u>:

Rent received in advance	understated by	$800
Retained earnings	overstated by	$800

QUIZ 1   CORRECTING CURRENT PERIOD DEFERRAL ERRORS

Problem I.

Multiple choice. Circle the correct answer.

1. You prepay rent for two years and debit Rent Expense. At the end of the current period, you will show the expense used up for the current period by:

    a. reducing Rent Expense
    b. increasing Rent Expense
    c. leaving Rent Expense unchanged
    d. reducing Prepaid Rent

2. You prepay rent for two years and debit Prepaid Rent. At the end of the current period, you will show the expense used up for the current period by:

    a. reducing Rent Expense
    b. leaving Rent Expense unchanged
    c. increasing Prepaid Rent
    d. reducing Prepaid Rent

3. On September 1, 20X1, your company paid $6,000 in advance to advertise in a local paper for the six months September 1, 20X1 – March 1, 20X2, and debited Advertising Expense. After the 20X1 books were closed, you discover that 20X1 Advertising Expense had not been adjusted at year end. Which of the following statements about the 20X1 accounts is true?

    a. 20X1 net income was understated by $6,000.
    b. Total assets are understated by $5,000.
    c. Prepaid Advertising is understated by $2,000.
    d. There is no error because only income statement accounts are affected.

4. On October 1, 20X0, your company rented office space for $1,000 a month and received a check for $6,000 for the first six months' rent. You recorded the $6,000 as rent revenue. On December 31, 20X0, an adjusting entry was made debiting Rent Revenue and crediting Rent Received in Advance for $4,000. Which of the following statements about the 20X0 accounts is true?

    a. All accounts are correctly stated.
    b. 20X0 net income is overstated by $1,000.
    c. 20X0 liabilities at year end are overstated by $1,000.
    d. 20X0 assets are correctly stated.

5. Deferral errors affect:

    a. both the income statement and balance sheet
    b. only the income statement
    c. only the balance sheet
    d. different statements depending upon the particular deferral

Problem II.

Fill in the blanks.

1. If you initially record revenue received in advance in a revenue account, the subsequent adjusting entry would _____ the revenue account and _____ a _____ account.

2. A deferred expense is one in which cash is _____ before it is _____ as an expense.

3. When your company makes a prepayment, you credit Cash, but you can debit either a(n) _____ account or a pre-paid _____ account.

4. When an advance payment is recorded to an expense account, to figure out the year-end adjustment, ask: "By what amount must the _____ account balance be _____ to show only the amount used up in the current period?"

5. When you have made an advance payment and recorded it in a prepaid account, to figure out the year-end adjustment, ask: "How much of the _____ _____ account balance must be transferred to the _____ account to show the amount used up in the current period?"

Problem III.

1. On July 1, 20X0, your company took out a four-year insurance policy at $2,000 per year. It prepaid the entire $8,000, recording it as a *prepayment*. Just before the books were closed, you discovered that the year-end AJE had mistakenly debited Insurance Expense for $6,000 and credited Prepaid Insurance. Show the correcting entry on December 31, 20X0.

2. On August 1, 20X0, your company prepaid six months of advertising expense for $9,000, which you recorded in Advertising Expense. On December 31 before the books are closed, you discover that the adjusting entry made at year end mistakenly debited Prepaid Advertising $4,000 and credited Advertising Expense for $4,000. Show the correcting entry on December 31, 20X0 before the books are closed.

3. On December 1, 20X0, your company sublets space for $900 per month. You received a check for $3,600 for four months' rent in advance—December, January, February, and March—that you recorded as *revenue*. Just before the books were closed, you discovered that the year-end AJE mistakenly debited Rent Revenue for $900 and credited Rent Received in Advance for $900. Show the correcting entry on 12/31/20X0.

4. On November 1, 20X0, your company receives an advance of $7,200 for a six-month consulting engagement, which you record in Unearned Consulting Revenue. Just before the books are closed on December 31, you discover that the year-end adjusting entry mistakenly debited Consulting Revenue for $2,400 and credited Unearned Consulting Revenue for $2,400. Show the correcting entry before the books are closed.

QUIZ 1 *Solutions and Explanations*

Problem I.

    1. a

    2. d

    3. c

    4. c

    5. a

Problem II.

    1. decrease or debit; increase or credit; liability

    2. paid; recognized

    3. expense; asset

    4. expense; reduced

    5. prepaid asset; expense

Problem III.

1. To compute insurance expense for 20X0: $2,000 per year x 6/12 (6 months of the year from January to June, 20X0) = $1,000 insurance expense used up in 20X0.

The correcting entry on 12/31/20X0 (before the books are closed) is:

Prepaid Insurance	5,000	
Insurance Expense		5,000

This entry leaves the correct Insurance Expense balance of $1,000 ($6,000 balance from AJE – $5,000 reduction from correcting entry = $1,000 correct balance) and leaves the correct amount of $7,000 in Prepaid Insurance to be deferred for future use ($2,000 balance after AJE + $5,000 increase = $7,000 correct balance).

2. To compute advertising expense on December 31, 20X0: $9,000 prepayment/6 months = $1,500 per month x 5 months = $7,500.

To compute prepaid advertising on December 31, 20X0: $9,000 prepayment – $7,500 expense incurred = $1,500 prepaid advertising.

The original AJE should have reduced Advertising Expense by $1,500 to leave a balance of $7,500. But the incorrect AJE reduced the account by $4,000, leaving a balance of only $5,000. To restore the correct balance in Advertising Expense of $7,500, you must add back $2,500.

The correcting entry on December 31, 20X0 (before the books are closed) is:

Advertising Expense	2,500	
Prepaid Advertising		2,500

This entry also leaves the correct Prepaid Advertising balance of $1,500. To compute: $4,000 balance from incorrect AJE – $2,500 from correcting entry = $1,500 correct balance. To prove this balance: $9,000 recorded in Advertising Expense when the prepayment was made – $7,500 expense actually incurred for 20X0 = $1,500 deferred for future use in the Prepaid Advertising account.

3. The correcting entry on 12/31/20X0 (before the books are closed) is:

Rent Revenue   1,800
    Rent Received in Advance   1,800

This entry leaves the correct balance in Rent Revenue of $900 ($2,700 balance remaining after AJE – $1,800 reduction = $900 correct balance) and defers the correct amount of $2,700 to Rent Received in Advance ($900 balance from incorrect AJE + $1,800 added back = $2,700 correct balance) to be earned in future periods. For more details, see Figure 5-9 (on page 101).

4. To compute consulting revenue earned for 20X0: $7,200 prepayment/6 months = $1,200 a month x 2 months (November and December) = $2,400 consulting revenue earned in 20X0.

To compute correct year-end balance in Unearned Revenue: $7,200 prepayment – $2,400 earned = $4,800 correct year-end balance.

To compute the reduction needed in Unearned Consulting Revenue: $7,200 balance + $2,400 incorrect AJE = $9,600 incorrect year-end balance – $4,800 correct year-end balance = $4,800 reduction needed in year-end balance.

The correcting entry on December 31, 20X0 (before the books are closed) is:

Unearned Consulting Revenue   4,800
    Consulting Revenue   4,800

This entry also leaves the correct balance of $2,400 in Consulting Revenue ($4,800 credit from correcting entry credit – $2,400 debit from incorrect AJE = $2,400 correct credit balance).

QUIZ 2   CORRECTING CURRENT PERIOD DEFERRAL ERRORS

Problem I.

Multiple choice. Circle the correct answer.

1. In December, your company sublets space and receives payment for four months in advance—December, January, February and March—crediting Rent Revenue for the full payment. On December 31, you show the revenue earned for the current period by:

    a. reducing Rent Revenue
    b. increasing Rent Revenue
    c. leaving Rent Revenue unchanged
    d. reducing Rent Received in Advance

2. In December, your company sublets space and receives payment for four months in advance—December, January, February and March—crediting Rent Received in Advance for the full payment. On December 31, you show the revenue earned for the current period by:

    a. reducing Rent Received in Advance
    b. increasing Rent Received in Advance
    c. leaving Rent Received in Advance unchanged
    d. reducing Rent Expense

3. Your company sells 500 season tickets for $100 each for 10 home hockey games to be played from November through March and credits the $50,000 to Ticket Sales Revenue. Four home games were played in 20X1, and 6 are to be played in 20X2. Just before the 20X1 books are closed on December 31, 20X1, you discover that Ticket Sales Revenue has not been adjusted at year end. As a result:

    a. 20X1 revenue is overstated
    b. too little revenue from the tickets is deferred for future use
    c. the correction requires a $30,000 credit to Unearned Ticket Revenue
    d. all of the above

Problem II.

Fill in the blanks.

1. Deferred revenue is cash _____ before it is recognized as _____.

2. When your company receives a prepayment, you debit Cash, but you can credit either a(n) _____ account or a(n) _____ account.

3. To compute the year-end adjustment for deferred revenue when you recorded the advance payment in a revenue account, ask: "By what amount must the _____ account balance be _____ to show only the amount earned for the current period?"

4. When you have recorded receipt of an advance payment in a liability account, to compute the year-end adjustment for deferred revenue, ask: "How much of the _____ account balance must be transferred to the _____ account to show the amount earned in the current period?"

Problem III.

1. When LeaseCo receives rent in advance, it credits Rent Revenue. On December 1, 20X1 it received $3,000 for three months' rent in advance, but never made an entry to recognize the amount earned in 20X1. This error was discovered after the books were closed.

   a. Show how this error affected LeaseCo's 20X1 financial statements.
   b. Give the correcting entry that must be made if the error is discovered before the books are closed.

2. On December 1, 20X0, your law firm received a retainer of $1,500—$300 per month for the next five months—that you recorded as *revenue*. Just before the books were closed, you discovered that the year-end AJE debited Revenue for $300 and credited to Fees Received in Advance for $300. Show the correcting entry.

3. Using the same facts as in question 2, show how this error would affect the 20X0 financial statements if it were not corrected.

4. On October 1, 20X0, your company took advantage of a special offer. You paid a trade magazine $24,000 for 12 monthly ads (one year) in advance, recording the entire amount as an *expense*. Just before the books were closed, you discovered that the AJE credited Advertising Expense for $22,000 and debited Prepaid Advertising for $22,000. Show the correcting entry.

5. Using the same facts as in question 4, show how this error would affect the 20X0 financial statements if it were not corrected.

QUIZ 2   Solutions and Explanations

Problem I.

    1. a

    2. a

    3. d
       To compute: $500 per game x 10 games played in 20X1 = $20,000 revenue earned in 20X1. $50,000 prepayment – $20,000 earned in 20X1 = $30,000 that should be credited to Unearned Ticket Revenue.

Problem II.

    1. received, revenue

    2. revenue, liability

    3. revenue, reduced

    4. liability (or unearned revenue or revenue received in advance), revenue

Problem III.

1. a. The error affects LeaseCo's 20X1 financial statements as follows:

    20X1 income statement:

Rent revenue	overstated by	$2,000
Net income	overstated by	$2,000

    20X1 balance sheet:

Unearned rent revenue	understated by	$2,000
Retained earnings	overstated by	$2,000

    b. The correcting entry before the books are closed is:

Rent Revenue	2,000	
Unearned Rent (or Rent Received in Advance)		2,000

2. The correcting entry is:

Revenue	900	
Fees Received in Advance		900

    This entry leaves the correct Revenue balance of $300 ($1,200 balance after AJE – $900 reduction = $300 correct remaining balance) and defers the correct amount of $1,200 to Fees Received in Advance ($300 balance from AJE + $900 addition = $1,200 correct balance) to be earned in future periods. See Figure 5-10 (on page 109) for more details.

3. Because the entire $1,500 prepaid fee was originally recorded in Revenue, at year end the AJE should have reduced Revenue by $1,200 to leave a balance of $300, the amount that your law firm actually earned for the year. Instead, the incorrect AJE reduced Revenue by only $300, leaving an incorrect year-end balance of $1,200. And because the year-end balance in Revenue was $900 too high, the year-end balance in Fees Received in Advance was $900 too low.

    Therefore, the effect of the error on the 20X0 income statement if it is not corrected is:

Revenue	overstated by	$900
Net income	overstated by	$900

    The effect of the error on the 20X0 balance sheet if it is not corrected is:

Fees received in advance	understated by	$900
Retained earnings	overstated by	$900

4. The correcting entry before the books were closed is:

Advertising Expense	4,000	
Prepaid Advertising		4,000

    This entry leaves the correct Advertising Expense balance of $6,000 ($2,000 balance after AJE + $4,000 added back = $6,000 correct balance) and defers the correct amount of $18,000 to Prepaid Advertising ($22,000 balance after AJE – $4,000 reduction = $18,000 correct balance to cover 9 months' [January–September] advertising expense in 20X1). For more details, see Figure 5-3 (on page 102).

5. Because the entire $24,000 in prepaid advertising was originally recorded in Advertising Expense, at year end, the AJE should have reduced this account by $18,000 to leave a balance of $6,000, the expense actually incurred for the year. To compute: $24,000/12 months = $2,000 advertising expense per month x 3 months (October, November, December) = $6,000 advertising expense incurred for the year. Instead, the incorrect AJE reduced Advertising Expense by $22,000. leaving an incorrect year-end balance of $2,000, which was $4,000 too low and a year-end balance in Prepaid Advertising that was $4,000 too high.

Thus, the effect of the error on the 20X0 income statement if it is not corrected is:

Advertising expense	understated by	$4,000
Net income	overstated by	$4,000

The effect of the error on the 20X0 balance sheet if it is not corrected is:

Prepaid advertising	overstated by	$4,000
Retained earnings	overstated by	$4,000

MASTERING CORRECTION OF ACCOUNTING ERRORS

Instructions: Select the letter that represents the best answer to each multiple choice question below and mark it on the Answer Sheet (page 141). Ignore tax effects. Allow approximately 2½ hours.

1. While reviewing a trial balance, you notice the following account balances. Which one is likely to be an error?

    a. Inventory with a debit balance of $43,000
    b. Discount on Bonds Payable with a debit balance of $4,000
    c. Accumulated Depreciation with a debit balance of $8,000
    d. Allowance for Doubtful Accounts with a credit balance of $23,000

2. Debiting an insurance payment to Rent Expense instead of Insurance Expense is an example of . . .

    a. an accrual error
    b. a deferral error
    c. a classification error
    d. use of an incorrect accounting principle

3. InCo. recorded a customer's $20,000 check as a $20,000 debit to Cash and as a $2,000 credit to Accounts Receivable. This is an example of:

    a. an oversight
    b. an incorrect account classification
    c. a transposition error
    d. a slide error

4. During a bank reconciliation, a deposit recorded by the bank but not in the company's ledger Cash account is . . .

    a. added to both the bank balance and the ledger Cash account balance
    b. added to the ledger Cash account balance only
    c. added to the bank balance only
    d. subtracted from the bank balance and added to the ledger Cash account balance

5. The bank statement balance of $7,000 does not include a check outstanding of $1,000, a deposit in transit of $275, and another company's $250 check erroneously charged against your firm's account. The reconciled bank balance is:

a. $6,375   b. $6,580   c. $6,525   d. $6,570

Use the following information to answer questions 6–8. You are doing a bank reconciliation for May, 20X1. You have a $2,785 unadjusted ledger cash balance and the following data:

- Outstanding checks: No. 719, $200; No. 727, $800; No. 732, $625
- Deposits in transit, $1,200
- Check No. 742 (for repairs) written for $505 but incorrectly recorded as $550
- NSF check from a customer, $500
- Bank service charge for May, $5
- Balance per bank statement, $2,750

6. What dollar amount should be deducted from the balance per bank statement?

a. $1,425   b. $1,625   c. $505   d. $2,125

7. What dollar amount should be deducted from the balance per books?

a. $460   b. $505   c. $550   d. $1,625

8. Which adjustment will you need to make to company books?

a. a net decrease in Cash of $550
b. a net decrease in Cash of $505
c. a net decrease in Cash of $460
d. a net increase in Cash of $45

9. Which of the following errors would *not* be revealed by the trial balance?

   a. a sale debited to Accounts Receivable for $500 and credited to Sales for $50
   b. a rent check debited to Rent Expense for $975 and credited to Cash for $795
   c. collection of a receivable debited to Cash for $300 and credited to Accounts Payable for $300
   d. payment of an account debited to Accounts Payable for $1,000 and debited to Cash for $1,000

10. A trial balance has total debits of $197,900 and total credits of $199,700. Which account may contain a transposition error?

   a. A Cash account with a balance of $900
   b. An Accounts Receivable with a balance of $1,800
   c. A Cost of Goods Sold account with a balance of $4,200
   d. An Accounts Payable with a balance of $5,300

Use the following trial balance to answer question 11.

	Debits	Credits
Cash	$ 10	
Accounts Receivable, net	20	
Inventory	50	
Long-term Investment	100	
Equipment	520	
Accumulated Depreciation		$200
Accounts Payable		20
Bond Payable		100
Discount on Bond Payable		10
Capital Stock		200
Retained Earnings		120
Revenues		310
Expenses	240	
Totals	$940	$960

11. Which account balance is listed in the wrong column?

   a. Cash
   b. Accounts Receivable
   c. Accounts Payable
   d. Discount on Bonds Payable
   e. Retained Earnings

12. Which account should not appear on a post-closing trial balance?

    a. Sales
    b. Retained Earnings
    c. Accumulated Depreciation
    d. Discount on Bonds Payable

13. Which of these errors is easiest to find and correct?

    a. failure to record a transaction
    b. crediting Sales Revenue instead of Accounts Receivable for a payment
    c. the Accumulated Depreciation balance in the debit column of a trial balance
    d. incorrect computation of the Notes Payable account balance

14. In November, 20X0, your company sublets space for $500 and receives advance rent of $1,500 for three months—November, December and January—that is credited to Rent Revenue. Before the 20X0 books are closed, you discover that at year-end, 20X0, no adjusting entry was made to Rent Revenue. To correct this omission . . .

    a. Rent Revenue should be debited for $500.
    b. Rent Revenue should be debited for $1,000.
    c. Rent Revenue should be debited for $1,500.
    d. Rent Received in Advance should be credited for $1,000.

15. In early November, 20X0, your company makes a $4,500 advance payment for six months' insurance and debits Prepaid Insurance for the entire amount. Before the books are closed for the year, you discover that no adjusting entry has been made. To correct this error, you will . . .

    a. debit Insurance Expense for $3,000
    b. credit Insurance Expense for $3,000
    c. debit Insurance Expense for $1,500
    d. debit Prepaid Insurance for $1,500

16. The Allowance for Doubtful Accounts . . .

    a. has a normal debit balance
    b. has a normal credit balance
    c. appears only on the post-closing trial balance
    d. any of the above

17. Which of the following might produce an account balance that is not normal?

    a. underpayment of an account payable
    b. overpayment of an account receivable by a customer
    c. underaccrual of interest expense
    d. none of the above

18. In a trial balance, if the total debits do not equal the total credits and the difference is divisible by 2, the error could be the result of . . .

    a. adding or deleting one or more zeros to or from an amount
    b. reversing two digits
    c. omitting an account balance
    d. showing a debit balance as a credit or a credit balance as a debit

19. Early in 20X2, while the 20X1 books are still open, you are informed that 20X1 Advertising Expense includes $90,000 for printing catalogs for a campaign to begin in January, 20X2 and that a $50,000 invoice for television commercials shown in December, 20X1 was debited to 20X2 Advertising Expense.

The correcting entry to record as of December 31, 20X1 is . . .

    a. a net debit to Advertising Expense of $50,000
    b. a net credit to Advertising Expense of $40,000
    c. a net credit to Advertising Expense of $90,000
    d. a net credit to Advertising Expense of $140,000

Use the following information to answer questions 20 and 21.

On January 1, 20X1 CleanCo credited Revenue for a $4,000 prepayment it received from a customer for maintenance services to be provided over the next two years.

20. If Revenue is not adjusted as of December 31, 20X1 . . .

    a. assets will be overstated by $2,000

    b. net income will be understated by $2,000

    c. revenues will be overstated by $2,000

    d. retained earnings will be understated by $2,000

21. An adjusting entry is necessary as of December 31, 20X1 to properly reflect . . .

    a. the ledger Cash account balance

    b. deferred revenue

    c. correction of the expense accrual

    d. accrual of expense

Use the following information to answer questions 22–24.

On July 1, 20X0, CriCo takes out a 10%, $10,000 note payable that is due on July 1, 20X1. No interest is accrued at year-end 20X0.

22. If the error is not discovered until July 1, 20X1 . . .

    a. it will require a prior period adjustment

    b. it will require a current period adjustment

    c. it will require both a and b

    d. it will require no correction

23. If no corrections are made, which of the following statements is correct?

    a. On CriCo's 20X0 income statement, net income is understated by $500.

    b. On CriCo's 20X0 income statement, net income is overstated by $500.

    c. On CriCo's 20X0 balance sheet, retained earnings is understated by $500.

    d. On CriCo's 20X0 balance sheet, liabilities are overstated by $500.

24. To correct this error in 20X0, you need to record just the adjusting entry that was not made because . . .

    a. an expense account is involved
    b. no error was made recording the note payable on July 1, 20X0
    c. an accrual is involved rather than a deferral
    d. the books have not been closed

25. If a check written by the company is recorded for the wrong amount, the error is likely to be found because . . .

    a. the trial balance will be out of balance by an amount divisible by 9
    b. the trial balance will be out of balance by an amount divisible by 2
    c. the bank reconciliation will be out of balance when the check clears
    d. the balance sheet will be out of balance

26. On October 1, 20X1, MarCo signs a one-year, 8% note payable for $10,000 with principle and interest due on October 1, 20X2. It is MarCo's only note outstanding. On October 1, 20X2 when the note is paid, MarCo debits Notes Payable and credits Cash for $10,800, the sum of principle and interest. This error is likely to be found because . . .

    a. the bank reconciliation will be out of balance when the check clears
    b. the trial balance will be out of balance by $800
    c. the trial balance will show a balance in Notes Payable that is not normal
    d. interest expense will be understated

27. While writing a check for $2,000 on April 26, 20X2 for a computer purchased on December 26, 20X1, you discover that when the purchase was made in December, the $2,000 had been credited to Notes Payable instead of Accounts Payable. If the books are closed, what single entry could you make?

a. Notes Payable	2,000	
Accounts Payable		2,000
b. Notes Payable	2,000	
Cash		2,000
c. Accounts Payable	2,000	
Cash		2,000
d. Accounts Payable	2,000	
Notes Payable		2,000

28. At year end, a physical count of office supplies reveals that $7,000 of supplies were used up but no adjusting entry was made to account for this. If this error is found, it will most likely be because . . .

    a. the trial balance would be out of balance by $7,000
    b. the trial balance would be out of balance by $14,000
    c. the trial balance would be out of balance by $3,500
    d. none of the above

29. If the omission in question 28 is found before the books are closed, the adjusting entry to correct the error will include . . .

    a. a debit to Office Supplies Expense
    b. a credit to Office Supplies Expense
    c. a debit to Inventory
    d. none of the above

30. The type of error given in question 28 is known as . . .

    a. a deferral error
    b. an accrual error
    c. a prior period error
    d. none of the above

31. OutCo failed to record depreciation on certain machinery for 20X1. This error . . .

    a. affects the income statement only
    b. affects the balance sheet only
    c. affects both the income statement and the balance sheet
    d. affects neither the income statement nor the balance sheet

32. Preventing or discovering accounting errors requires knowing and using . . .

    a. double-entry bookkeeping
    b. internal controls
    c. inspection of the trial balance
    d. all of the above

33. On July 1, 20X1, a machine is purchased at a cost of $20,000. Before the 20X1 books are closed you discover that an error caused by using an incorrect residual value resulted in depreciation for the year being $200 too high. To correct this error you will record a second adjusting entry for depreciation that will include . . .

    a. a $200 debit to Depreciation Expense
    b. a $200 credit to Asset—Machinery
    c. a $200 debit to Accumulated Depreciation
    d. none of the above

34. The post-closing trial balance should be reviewed to make sure that . . .

    a. Retained Earnings has the ending and not the beginning balance
    b. only balance sheet accounts remain open
    c. all temporary accounts and their contra accounts have been closed out
    d. all of the above

35. Before the 20X1 books are closed, you discover that on January 2, 20X1, when a new machine was purchased for $20,000, the $20,000 was debited to Machinery Maintenance Expense. The new machine, which is being depreciated under the straight-line method, has a 10-year life and no estimated salvage value. However, because of the error, no depreciation was recorded for the year. If no correction is made . . .

    a. net income for 20X1 will be understated by $18,000
    b. net income for 20X1 will be understated by $2,000
    c. total assets on the December 31, 20X1 balance sheet will be understated by $20,000
    d. the trial balance will not balance

36. The error described in question 35 is likely to be discovered because . . .

    a. inspection of the trial balance would reveal Machinery had a balance that was not normal
    b. inspection of the trial balance would reveal Machinery Maintenance Expense had an unusually large balance
    c. inspection of the trial balance would reveal no depreciation expense
    d. none of the above

37. You are given the following complete trial balance:

	Debits	Credits
Account A	$ 536	
Account B	727	
Account C	332	
Account D	447	
Account E		$1,044
Account F		322
Account G		218
Account H		894
	$2,042	$2,478

Which account appears to have its balance improperly transferred to the trial balance?

a. Account A   e. Account E
b. Account B   f. Account F
c. Account C   g. Account G
d. Account D   h. Account H

38. You are given the following complete trial balance with one account containing a transposition error:

	Debits	Credits
Account A	$ 354	
Account B	422	
Account C	1,073	
Account D	365	
Account E		$ 725
Account F		993
Account G		629
Account H		137
	$2,214	$2,484

Which account appears to contain the transposition error?

a. Account A   e. Account E
b. Account B   f. Account F
c. Account C   g. Account G
d. Account D   h. Account H

39. Which of the following is an example of an accrual error?

    a. failure to adjust Prepaid Insurance to its proper balance at year end

    b. failure to adjust Inventory to its proper balance at year end

    c. failure to record depreciation at year end

    d. none of the above

40. Which of the following is an example of a deferral error?

    a. initially recording advance payment of an insurance premium to Prepaid Insurance instead of Insurance Expense

    b. failure to record interest expense incurred but not yet paid

    c. failure to adjust Unearned Revenue to its proper balance at year end

    d. none of the above

41. On April 1, 20X0, your company finances partial payment of the sale of machinery to a customer for a $20,000, 3-year, 8% note receivable. Interest is payable annually on April 1. On December 31, 20X0, an adjusting entry debits Interest Receivable and credits Interest Revenue for $1,600. The entry necessary to correct the error before the books are closed would include . . .

    a. a $400 debit to Interest Revenue

    b. a $400 credit to Interest Expense

    c. a $400 credit to Unearned Interest Receivable

    d. a $400 credit to Sales

42. Which of the following statements about accrual and deferral errors is correct?

    a. Accrual errors affect only balance sheet accounts.

    b. Deferral errors affect only income statement accounts.

    c. Accrual and deferral errors affect both income statement and balance sheet accounts.

    d. All above statements are correct.

43. When preparing 20X2 financial statements, you discover that depreciation expense was not recorded in 20X1. Which of the following statements about correction of the error in 20X2 is *not* true?

    a. The correction requires a prior period adjustment.

    b. The correcting entry will be different than if the error had been corrected the previous year when it occurred.

    c. The 20X1 Depreciation Expense account will be involved in the correcting entry.

    d. All above statements are true.

44. Which of the following is an accurate description of how failure to record an accrual is likely to be found?

    a. An expense that was not accrued is paid, but there is no payable on the books as there should be.

    b. A revenue that was not accrued is received, but there is no receivable on the books as there should be.

    c. A review of the trial balance reveals that an asset or liability account that is normally present after accruals are recorded is not present.

    d. All above statements are accurate descriptions of how failure to record an accrual is likely to be found.

45. A comparison of this year's trial balance with last year's may be a good way to discover . . .

    a. whether normal accruals were made this year

    b. whether normal deferrals were made this year

    c. errors in accruals or deferrals that have resulted in over- or under-statement of revenues or expenses

    d. all of the above

46. When trying to find errors in a trial balance that does not balance, the first step should be to . . .

    a. work from the ledger to the trial balance to check the journal entries and postings for errors

    b. see if the ledger account balances have been calculated correctly

    c. work from the ledger to the trial balance to verify that ledger account balances were transferred to the correct debit or credit columns

    d. work from the trial balance to the ledger to verify that ledger account balances were transferred to the correct debit or credit columns

47. Which of the following is *not* a normal balance?

  a. a $6,000 credit balance in Discount on Bonds Payable
  b. a $9,000 credit balance in Unearned Service Revenue
  c. a $1,200 debit balance in Sales Returns and Allowances
  d. a $10,000 debit balance in Treasury Stock

48. Which of the following uncorrected errors would result in both assets and net income being overstated?

  a. failure to adjust Unearned Revenue to recognize revenue earned
  b. failure to record depreciation for the year
  c. failure to accrue interest payable
  d. adjusting Prepaid Insurance by crediting it for an amount that is too large

49. If trial balance total debits are $72,000 and total credits are $74,700, then the error can*not* be . . .

  a. a slide
  b. a doubling error
  c. a transposition for which you can find the error by investigating each account where the difference between the first two digits of its balance is 3
  d. Actually, you *can* find the error using a, b or c.

50. In your trial balance, total debits are $264,000 and total credits are $259,500. You have determined that the error may be a transposition and that you may find the error by investigating accounts with balances for which the difference between the first two digits is 5. Which of the following account balances could be the problem?

  a. Accounts Receivable, with an indicated balance of $1,600
  b. Accounts Payable, with an indicated balance of $1,600
  c. Land, with an indicated balance of $4,900
  d. both a and c

Final Examination Answer Sheet

MASTERING CORRECTION OF ACCOUNTING ERRORS

Instructions: Detach this sheet before starting the Final Exam. For each question, check the box beneath the letter of the correct answer. Use a #2 pencil to make a dark impression. When completed, return to: AIPB Continuing Education, Suite 500, 6001 Montrose Road, Rockville, MD 20852. If you attain a grade of at least 70, you will receive the Institute's *Certificate of Completion*. Answer Sheets are not returned.

Certified Bookkeeper applicants: If you attain a grade of at least 70, and become certified within 3 years of passing this exam, you will receive retroactively seven (7) Continuing Professional Education Credits (CPECs) toward your *Certified Bookkeeper* CPEC requirements.

1. a b c d
2. a b c d
3. a b c d
4. a b c d
5. a b c d
6. a b c d
7. a b c d
8. a b c d
9. a b c d
10. a b c d
11. a b c d e
12. a b c d
13. a b c d

14. a b c d
15. a b c d
16. a b c d
17. a b c d
18. a b c d
19. a b c d
20. a b c d
21. a b c d
22. a b c d
23. a b c d
24. a b c d
25. a b c d
26. a b c d

27. a b c d
28. a b c d
29. a b c d
30. a b c d
31. a b c d
32. a b c d
33. a b c d
34. a b c d
35. a b c d
36. a b c d
37. a b c d
   e f g h

38. a b c d
   e f g h
39. a b c d
40. a b c d
41. a b c d
42. a b c d
43. a b c d
44. a b c d
45. a b c d
46. a b c d
47. a b c d
48. a b c d
49. a b c d
50. a b c d

Name _____ Title _____

Company _____ Street Address _____

City _____ State _____ Zip _____

For *Certified Bookkeeper* applicants only: #_____
Membership or Certification (nonmember) ID Number

Course Evaluation for

MASTERING CORRECTION OF ACCOUNTING ERRORS

Please complete and return (even if you do not take the Final Examination) to: AIPB Continuing Education, Suite 500, 6001 Montrose Road, Rockville, MD 20852. **PLEASE PRINT CLEARLY.**

Circle one

1. Did you find the instructions clear? Yes No
Comments: _____

2. Did you find the course practical? Yes No
Comments_____

3. Is this course what you expected? Yes No
Comments_____

4. Would you recommend this course to other accounting professionals? Yes No
Comments: _____

5. What did you like most about *Mastering Correction of Accounting Errors*? _____

6. What would have made the course even more helpful? _____

7. May we use your comments and name in advertising for the course? Yes No

8. Would you be interested in other courses? Yes No

Please indicate what subject areas would be of greatest interest to you:

1. _____   4. _____
2. _____   5. _____
3. _____   6. _____

_____   _____
Name (optional)   Title

_____   _____
Company   Street Address

_____   _____
City   State   Zip   Phone Number

NOTES

NOTES